Leckie
the education publisher
for Scotland

National 5
ENGLISH

For SQA 2019 and beyond

D1580691

Revision + Practice
2 Books in 1

ISBN 9780008435332

Published by
Leckie
An imprint of HarperCollinsPublishers
Westerhill Road, Bishopbriggs, Glasgow, G64 2QT
T: 0844 576 8126   F: 0844 576 8131
leckiescotland@harpercollins.co.uk   www.leckiescotland.co.uk

Publisher: Sarah Mitchell
Project Manager: Harley Griffiths and Lauren Murray

Special thanks to
QBS (layout and illustration)

Printed in Italy by Grafica Veneta S.p.A

A CIP Catalogue record for this book is available from the British Library.

Acknowledgements
Extracts: pp. 35–36: Copyright Guardian News & Media Ltd 2018; p.37: © Matthew Syed, The Times / News Licensing, 19/01/2015; pp. 38–39: Tom Lamont / Copyright Guardian N ews & Media Ltd 2018; pp. 40–41: Hartswood Films/Steven Moffat; pp. 42–43: Danny Baker /Orion Books; p.48: Yuval Noah Harari; pp. 51–53: Simon Parkin / Copyright Guardian News & Media Ltd 2018; pp. 60–61: Jonathan Jones / Copyright Guardian News & Media Ltd 2018; pp. 70–72: Rona Munro / Hodder Education; pp. 73–74: Iain Crichton Smith / Birlinn Ltd; pp. 76–77: Anne Donovan / Canongate Books; pp. 79–80: Robert Louis Stevenson; p.83: Carol Ann Duffy / Picador; p.85: Edwin Morgan / Carcanet Press; p.87: Norman MacCaig / Birlinn Ltd – reproduced with permission of the Licensor through PLSclear

pp. 112–113, extract from Land Rover: The Story of the Car that Conquered the World by Ben Fogle. Reprinted by permission of HarperCollins Publishers Ltd © 2016, Ben Fogle; pp 146–147, extract from Diversify by June Sarpong. Reprinted by permission of HarperCollins Publishers Ltd © 2017, June Sarpong; pp. 116–117, 150–151, extracts from Bold Girls by Rona Munro were reproduced by permission of Nick Hern Books © 1995, Rona Munro; pp 120–121, 154–155 extracts from Tally's Blood by Anne-Marie Di Mambro were reproduced by permission of Hodder Education © 2002, Ann- Marie Di Mambro; pp 118–119, extract from Sailmaker by Alan Spence was reproduced by permission of Hodder Education © 1988, Alan Spence; pp. 129–131, 162–163 extracts from Home, The Red Door and Mother and Son by Iain Crichton Smith were reproduced by permission of Birlinn Ltd through PLSclear © 2001, Iain Crichton Smith; pp 131–132, 164–165 extracts from Hieroglyphics, All That Glisters and Dear Santa by Anne Donovan were reproduced by permission of Canongate Books © 2004, Anne Donovan; pp 125–126, 160–161, extracts from The Testament of Gideon Mack by James Robertson on were reproduced by permission of Penguin Books Ltd © 2007, James Robertson; pp 123–25, 156–157, extracts from The Cone-Gatherers by Robin Jenkins were reproduced by permission of Canongate Books; pp 133, 156, the poems 'In Mrs Tilscher's Class', 'The Way My Mother Speaks' and 'Mrs Midas' from Collected Poems by Carol Ann Duffy. Published by Picador, 2015. Copyright © Carol Ann Duffy. Reproduced by permission of the author c/o Rogers, Coleridge & White Ltd., 20 Powis Mews, London W111JN; pp 139–141, 172–173 the poems 'Old Tongue', 'Whilst Leila Sleeps' and 'Gap Year (for Mateo)' from Darling: New & Selected Poems by Jackie Kay. Reproduced by permission of Bloodaxe Books, on behalf of the publisher. www.bloodaxebooks.com; pp 137–38, 170–171, the poems 'Brooklyn Cop', 'Assisi' and 'Hotel Room, 12th Floor' by Norman MacCaig were reproduced by permission of Birlinn Ltd through PLSclear © 2018, Norman MacCaig; pp135–36, 168–169, 'Glasgow 5th March 1971', 'Winter' and 'Glasgow Sonnet' by Edwin Morgan were reproduced by permission of Carcanet Press Ltd.;

Questions and information on pages: 24, 25, 34, 36, 39, 44, 64, 67, 68, 90 © Scottish Qualifications Authority

Images: p.8 Hemera; p.9(tr) lightpoet; p.9(cl) chbaum / Shutterstock; p.9(cr) Ulmus Media / Shutterstock; p.9(bl) iStockphoto; p.9(br) iStockphoto; p.10(c) Monkey Business Images; p.10(b) iStockphoto; p.21 Lifesize; p.22 Digital Vision; p.25 Martina Osmy / Shutterstock; p.27 Image source; p.29 Scanrail1 / Shutterstock; p.35 antoniondiaz / Shutterstock; p.38 Guardian Newspapers/Ross Gilmore; p.40(l) Africa Studio / Shutterstock; p.40(r) Fotyma / Shutterstock; p.42 iStockphoto; p.47 tassel78 / Shutterstock; p.51 Prostock-studio / Shutterstock; p.60 jorisvo / Shutterstock; p.70 Strat Mastoris / NVT; p.73 Milos Luzanin; p.76 Pixel Memoirs; p.87 Gareth Lowndes / Shutterstock; p.89 Drakonova / Shutterstock; p.91(1) Elnur / Shutterstock; p.91(2) LanKS / Shutterstock; p.91(3) Mr.Heisenberg / Shutterstock; p.91(4) stockshoppe / Shutterstock; p.105 Catalin Petolea / Shutterstock

All other images © Shutterstock.com

Whilst every effort has been made to trace the copyright holders, in cases where this has been unsuccessful, or if any have inadvertently been overlooked, the Publishers would gladly receive any information enabling them to rectify any error or omission at the first opportunity.

ebook

To access the ebook version of this Revision Guide visit
www.collins.co.uk/ebooks
and follow the step-by-step instructions.

Contents

Contents

Chapter 4: The question paper: critical reading

Chapter 5: More study and revision advice 104

Part 2: Practice exam papers

ANSWERS Check your answers to the practice exam papers online: www.leckieandleckie.co.uk

Introduction

Complete Revision and Practice

This Complete **two-in-one Revision and Practice** book is designed to support you as students of National 5 English. It can be used either in the classroom, for regular study and homework, or for exam revision. By combining **a revision guide and two full sets of practice exam papers**, this book includes everything you need to be fully familiar with the National 5 English exam. As well as including ALL the core course content with practice opportunities, there is comprehensive assignment and exam preparation advice, with both revision question and pratice exam paper answers provided online at www.leckieandleckie.co.uk.

National 5 English

National 5 English is one of the most important qualifications for candidates in Scottish schools today. The National 5 course gives you the opportunity to build on what you have already learned in the Broad General Education phase of Curriculum for Excellence and/or in National 4 English. It is a skills-based course that aims to develop your listening, talking, reading and writing skills (*literacy* skills and *thinking* skills). It will help to equip you with skills for life and with skills for work. These skills are fundamental to your future. Success at National 5 will increase the choices open to you in later life. Doing well at this level will allow you to get that job or training place you want; get access to college courses or progress to Higher English. This book will tell you all you need to know about how to pass assessments, create a good portfolio of writing, prepare for your exam and maximise your chances of success.

Course structure

National 5 English consists of four assessment components. These are:
- Reading for understanding, analysis and evaluation
- Critical reading
- Portfolio – writing
- Performance – spoken language

The first three of these are assessed externally by the SQA (in the exam) and your class teacher assesses the spoken language component in school.

Assessment

The exam consists of two papers.

The first paper is called **Reading for understanding, analysis and evaluation** and it is worth 30 marks. In this paper you will be asked to read **a passage of non-fiction prose** and then answer a series of **questions on the passage**. You should be familiar with this kind of 'close reading' from your work in English during S1–S3 and/or in your National 4 course.

The second paper is called **Critical reading** and it has two parts. It is worth 40 marks. In the first part you will answer questions on a **Scottish text** you have studied as part of the National 5 course (20 marks). In the second part you will have to write one **critical essay** about a play, novel, short story, poem, non-fiction text, film or TV programme you have studied in class as part of the National 5 course (20 marks). You cannot use the same text in both parts and your answer in part 2 must cover a different genre from the text you answered on in part 1. We'll look at how that works in practice later in the book.

The **Portfolio – writing** is worth 30 marks. You will submit two pieces of writing to be marked by the SQA. One of the pieces has to be broadly **creative** (a story, a poem, a piece of drama, etc.). The other piece has to be broadly **discursive** (persuasive or argumentative). You will already have experience of these types of writing from your work in S1–S3 and/or at National 4. Due to the **Portfolio – writing** being worth 30% of your total mark, it is really important that you devote your time and energy to sending away the best material that you can. Remember, this is the one part of the assessment that is entirely under your control.

The **Performance – spoken language** component requires you to do **one** of the following:

'Take part in a group discussion, or discussion-based activity, to which they contribute relevant ideas, opinions, or information, using detailed language.'

or

'Prepare and present a presentation. The presentation must be detailed in content, and must be structured in a clear and relevant way. Candidates must answer questions from the audience at some point in the presentation.'[1]

This assessment component is pass/fail only but you must pass in order to achieve a course award, no matter how well you do in the final exam!

[1]National 5 English Course Specification, SQA

Summary of assessment

Assessment component	Assessment type	Marks available	Time
Reading for understanding, analysis and evaluation	External exam paper	30	1 hour
Critical reading, part 1 Question on Scottish texts	External exam paper	20	1 hour 30 minutes
Critical reading, part 2 Critical essay	External exam paper	20	
Portfolio – writing	Coursework submitted to SQA	30 (15 marks each piece)	Completed during the session. Submitted in March.
Performance – spoken language	Internal assessment	Pass/fail only	Assessed on one occasion or over the course of the session.

LECKIE
the education publisher
for Scotland

National 5
ENGLISH

For SQA 2019 and beyond

Revision Guide

Iain Valentine

Talking and listening

Every day you spend in school you are involved in talking and listening in one form or another: talking to your pals on the way into the building; listening to bulletin notices being read out in registration; sharing ideas with other people in your group in the Modern Studies class; listening to your Maths teacher explain about quadratic equations; asking about something you don't understand in your homework. It's now very rare, apart from during exams and tests, for you **not** to be involved in these activities while you are in school. In fact, by the time you reach S4 and National 5 English, you've already got years of experience in talking and listening to others!

This means that achieving a pass in the Performance – spoken language component of the course is well within your capabilities. Some people, however, can still find it difficult or even a bit frightening to speak to an audience when they know they are being assessed. The trick is to always appear to be a confident individual – even when you don't always feel like that inside!

Resist the temptation to ask the teacher if you can 'come in during the lunch break and do my talk then'. Talking in front of an audience or as part of a group is one of the most important life skills you can acquire and develop during your time in school and it's no bad thing if this assessment takes you a wee bit out of your comfort zone.

Assessment

Let's look at what this assessment involves.

You can choose to take part in a group discussion or give a presentation to the class or small group.

If you take part in a group discussion it might be on one of the following:

- an issue in the news
- a local issue
- something that affects you and your classmates
- an aspect of one of the texts you are studying for the Critical reading paper (*Was Macbeth solely responsible for his downfall? What are the typical features of an Anne Donovan short story?*).

If you choose to prepare and deliver a presentation, it might be on one of the following:

- something you feel strongly about
- the topic you have chosen for your discursive writing
- an ambition you have
- an important event in history
- five suggestions you have to improve your school
- a person you admire.

The possibilities for both the discussion and the presentation are limitless. No matter which one you choose or get involved in, you must show you can:

- employ detailed and relevant ideas and/or information using a structure appropriate to purpose and audience
- communicate meaning effectively through the selection and use of detailed spoken language
- use aspects of non-verbal communication
- demonstrate listening skills by responding to spoken language.[2]

Your teacher will watch your performance and complete a detailed checklist as a record of the assessment.

Now let's look at each of the assessment criteria for this element of the course in more detail and think about what you have to do to achieve them. Remember that it is probably more straightforward than you think.

---

[2]SQA National 5 Course Specification

Assessment criteria		What you have to do	
		Group discussion	Presentation
Employs detailed and relevant ideas and/or information using a structure appropriate to purpose and audience	**Content** Can contribute a range of detailed and relevant ideas/views/opinions/information.	Get *involved* in the discussion. Get your ideas out there! Don't sit back and wait to be asked and don't just stop after saying one thing!	Make sure you have prepared enough material for the presentation. You'll probably need five or six main points to cover on your chosen topic.
	Structure Spoken language is structured effectively, and, where appropriate, takes account of the contributions of others.	Agree or disagree with what others say in the group. Give support where you can ('I think that's a good point, Ali.'). Ask direct questions of the others ('Why do you think that, Chris?').	Make sure there is an obvious introduction, development and conclusion to your talk – people often forget about the importance of *ending* the talk effectively.
	Relevance Attention to task, purpose and audience is sustained.	Stay on task. Resist any temptation to tell the group about your latest followers on Instagram if you're supposed to be talking about Carol Ann Duffy. Keep to the topic.	Stay on task. Stick to what you've set out to tell the audience about. Resist the temptation to make any comments or asides to (or about) anyone in your audience.
Communicates meaning effectively through the selection and use of detailed spoken language	**Choice and use of language** Can select and use detailed spoken language that is appropriate to purpose and audience.	If you have been asked to discuss a topic based on the literature you are studying, then you *can't avoid* using 'detailed language' – it would be impossible to talk about *Macbeth* or Carol Ann Duffy's poetry without using appropriate literary terminology such as 'character', 'theme' and 'symbol'. For other topics try to make sure you use the kind of vocabulary that is relevant and connected to the subject.	Use language connected to your subject. If possible make use of topic-specific vocabulary. If you have chosen to give a presentation on, say, whether or not zoos are a good idea, then words and terms such as 'captivity', 'enclosure', 'cruelty', 'environment', 'extinction' and 'breeding programme' might well feature in your talk. These would be good examples of the detailed vocabulary required in the assessment. Remember

			also that your choice of language should suit your audience, which is likely to be made up of your classmates and your teacher, in other words a group of reasonably intelligent individuals. So treat them as such!
	Clarity and accuracy Can employ appropriate spoken language with sufficient clarity and accuracy to ensure that effective communication is achieved.	This doesn't just refer to the sound of your voice and the way you pronounce your words; it's also a reminder to make sure that your ideas come across clearly to the others in the group. Don't speak too quickly!	This doesn't just refer to the sound of your voice and the way you pronounce your words; it's also a reminder to make sure that your ideas come across clearly to your audience. Pausing now and again can be very effective.
Uses aspects of non-verbal communication	Can employ appropriate non-verbal features to assist communication and/or meaning. These might include facial expression, emphasis, gesture, eye contact, etc.	Look around at the other members of the group as much as you can when you are speaking. Maintain eye contact with someone who is making a point – it will show you are interested in what they are saying. Smile. Nod in encouragement or shake your head when you don't agree with something. You might find yourself waving your hand about to emphasise a point or even banging on the table if things get heated – just make sure you don't overdo things.	Maintaining eye contact with your audience is really important. If you can't look them in the eye then look just above their heads. Don't keep looking around at the screen. Don't fidget as you stand in front of the audience – just try to be as natural as possible. Use hand gestures to emphasise a point if it feels right.

Assessment criteria		What you have to do	
		Group discussion	Presentation
Demonstrates listening skills by responding to detailed spoken language	Can give relevant responses to the contributions of others in group discussions or in a series of discussion-based activities. OR Can respond relevantly to questions which follow, for example an individual presentation.	You'll find yourself doing this automatically if you take a full part in the discussion, but just make sure you listen carefully to what the other people in the group are saying. Respond if someone asks you a direct question. You can also display your listening skills by summarising what someone else has said ('So what you're saying is …') or asking for clarification ('I get that point, David, but what about …?').	Ask for questions at the end of the talk. You'll need to answer two or three to provide sufficient evidence to meet this criterion. Always try to give as full a reply as possible. You might want to begin your replies with expressions such as 'I'm glad you asked me that' or 'That's a really good question'. Not only is this polite, it gives you a few extra moments to gather your thoughts before you answer.

While you are taking part in the discussion, your teacher will be assessing you and keeping a record of the evidence by completing a detailed checklist. Look at the example on the next two pages and you'll see the sort of things he or she is looking out for.

Performance – spoken language assessment checklist

Candidate name: Fiona Smith		Activity: Group discussion (Should pupils be offered a wider range of subjects in school?)

National 5 English: Performance – spoken language

Aspect of performance		Achieved/ not achieved	Assessor's comments
Employs detailed and relevant ideas and/or information using a structure appropriate to purpose and audience	**Content** Can contribute a range of detailed and relevant ideas/views/opinions/information.	✓	Makes a number of relevant points: • Unfairness of current situation • Suggests other subjects that should be made available to pupils • Gives examples from her previous school (Arabic, Coding) Challenges Hannah – 'No, I don't think that's right ...' and gives examples to support. Stays on task throughout.
	Structure Spoken language is structured effectively, and, where appropriate, takes account of the contributions of others.	✓	
	Relevance Attention to task, purpose and audience is sustained.	✓	
Communicates meaning effectively through the selection and use of detailed spoken language	**Choice and use of language** Can select and use detailed spoken language that is appropriate to purpose and audience.	✓	Appropriate vocabulary in evidence: • 'Arguably ...', 'curriculum', 'skills for life' • 'I see that, but what about equal opportunities?' Accurate and clear throughout.
	Clarity and accuracy Can employ appropriate spoken language with sufficient clarity and accuracy to ensure that effective communication is achieved.	✓	

Aspect of performance		Achieved/ not achieved	Assessor's comments
Uses aspects of non-verbal communication	Can employ appropriate non-verbal features to assist communication and/or meaning. These might include facial expression, emphasis, gesture, eye contact, etc.	✓	• Maintains eye contact with other members of the group • Alert facial expression throughout • Nods in agreement with Hannah's statement • Responds to question from Jake. • Answers in detail about her previous school.
Demonstrates listening skills by responding to detailed spoken language	Can give relevant responses to the contributions of others in group discussions or in a series of discussion-based activities. OR Can respond relevantly to questions which follow, for example an individual presentation.	✓	

Additional comments:

This was an impressive performance. Fiona made a good number of contributions. A clear pass.

Assessor name: Ms Anna Sessor	**Assessor signature:** Anna Sessor	**Date:** 23.11.19

Group discussion and individual talk: some further points

It is important that you remember the importance of 'turn taking' in a discussion. Don't talk over the other members of the group – make sure you take it in turns to speak. That doesn't mean that the discussion should just go around in a kind of circle:

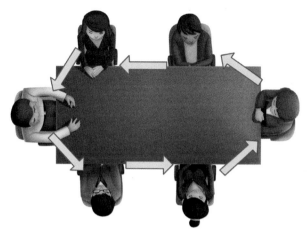

That can lead to a very dull kind of discussion. It is sometimes useful to go around the table to clarify what people's views are, but usually the best group discussion is much more complex as people summarise what others say; challenge their ideas; agree and disagree; and support points that are made. That sort of discussion looks like this:

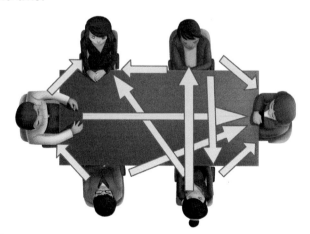

Using notes

If you have prepared your presentation thoroughly, then you should only need your notes to remind you about what to say next if you forget. They should be no more than bullet points of key ideas on a series of cue cards. If you are asked to talk to your audience about your ambitions for the future, your cue cards don't need to be any more complicated than these:

My ambition: to play for the Scotland women's national football team.
- why I love football
- playing at primary school
- seeing the Scotland team

- wanting to be like the players I admire
- my training regime
- getting a trial for Hibs Ladies

- going to apply to uni to do Sports Science – how to achieve this
- combine studying and playing football
- get picked for national squad

If you have prepared your presentation thoroughly, you should be able to talk for three or four minutes quite easily. Try it out at home first in front of a parent, or your sister, or the mirror.

You might also use notes in a group discussion if you have been given time for preparation before the activity.

Using slides

You might support your presentation by using slides (PowerPoint or Prezi or something similar) or by using props or other audiovisual aids. If you do use slides, don't forget the following:

*   don't have too much text on your slides
*   don't just read out what's on the slides to the audience
*   don't keep turning around to look at the screen.

And finally …

Don't worry if your presentation or your group discussion doesn't go as well as you had hoped it would, or if you didn't meet all the assessment criteria on this particular occasion. Your teacher can gather evidence for performance – spoken language from a number of talking and listening activities that you take part in during the course.

What you have to do

As well as sitting the question paper, you will have to send a portfolio of your best writing to the SQA for assessment.

You must submit two pieces of writing, each from a different genre. Each piece will be marked out of 15 and the total score out of 30 for the portfolio will be added to your marks from the question paper to decide your final grade of A, B, C, etc.

The writing pieces are your responsibility but they will be written under supervision and control. This means that you might submit a plan and a first draft to your teacher who will then make suggestions to help you improve your work. You would then take the piece away again and complete a final draft.

The work must be your own. You cannot copy content from elsewhere or have a teacher, tutor or parent write any of it for you. There are severe penalties for plagiarism. You must list any sources you have consulted in your writing (for example, give the URL address for websites).

Each piece should be no more than 1,000 words long (although the SQA operates a tolerance of 10%).

Each piece should be typed if possible and printed double-sided on the template you or your teacher can download from the SQA N5 web pages.

EXAM TIP

When you copy and paste your original piece of writing onto the SQA template, make sure your font, paragraphing, line spacing, etc. are all the way you want them to be. Make things easy for your marker and always use a simple font for the writing you send to the SQA.

- Times New Roman, Arial and Calibri are all suitable fonts
- 12 point is an effective font size to use (although your marker will be able to enlarge your script when they mark it online).

What the writing portfolio must contain

As stated above, your writing portfolio must contain **two** pieces of writing: a **creative** piece and a **discursive** piece.

The following table shows you which types of writing you can choose to do:

Group A – creative	Group B – discursive
A personal/reflective essay	A piece of transactional or informative writing
A piece of prose fiction (e.g. a short story, an episode from a novel)	A persuasive essay
A poem or set of thematically linked poems	An argumentative essay
A dramatic script (e.g. a scene, a monologue, a sketch)	A report for a specified purpose

You should already be familiar with most of these genres from your work in your Curriculum for Excellence English courses.

As long as you choose one category from Group A and one from Group B, your writing portfolio will be acceptable to the SQA. For example you might submit the following combinations:

- a short story and a persuasive piece on why all pupils should use smartphones in class
- a poem and a report on the time allocated to PE in Scottish schools
- a single-scene drama script and an argumentative essay that explores the topic of social media
- a reflective essay on why snowboarding is important to you and a transactional piece giving information on the discipline system used in your school.

EXAM TIP

This is the one element of your assessment that is entirely under your control. As it is worth 30% of your overall mark, it makes sense to put as much effort into this as you can. **Don't** allow yourself to hand in work that is not the best you can possibly do.

Let's look at how your writing pieces will be marked. Your marker will allocate each piece to a category and then decide on a final mark within that category. The table on the next page shows what the features of a **very good** piece of writing are (Category 1) as well as the features of a piece of writing that is **just good enough** to pass (Category 3).

Type of writing	Category 1 Essays in this category will be awarded 14 or 15 marks.	Category 3 Essays in this category will be awarded 8, 9 or 10 marks.
Discursive: information/ report	Information is presented to maximise impact and is carefully sequenced to highlight key points.	Information is presented in a clear sequence.
Discursive: persuasive/ argumentative	Ideas/techniques deployed to argue/discuss/persuade have sustained objectivity/ depth/complexity/insight and persuasive force, and are garnered, where appropriate, to convey a clear line of thought/ appropriate stance/point of view.	Ideas/techniques deployed to argue/discuss/persuade have some detail, can persuade the reader and convey a line of thought/ stance/point of view, although this might not be entirely consistent.
Creative: personal/ reflective	Feelings/reactions/ experiences are expressed/ explored with sustained involvement, insight and sensitivity.	Feelings/reactions/ experiences are rendered with a sense of involvement.
Creative: imaginative	The work displays some style, imagination and sophistication. The genre features of the chosen form are deployed skilfully.	The work is sound and there is evidence of mature thought. The genre features of the chosen form are deployed with varying degrees of success.
Relevance	Attention to purpose is consistently detailed.	Attention to purpose is well sustained.
Structure	Paragraphing and structure are very effective and enhance meaning/purpose.	A discernible structure is evident, but there are some lapses in paragraphing.
Technical accuracy	Sentence construction and punctuation are accurate, controlled and varied. Spelling is accurate. Very few formal errors.	Sentencing and punctuation are mostly accurate with some variety. Spelling is mainly accurate. Few formal errors.

Expression	Word choice is varied/apt/economical and creates particular effects.	Word choice supports meaning effectively, in the main.
	Meaning is clear at first reading.	Meaning is mostly clear at first reading.
Length	Substantial, but within the 1,000 word limit.	Within the word limit.
Overall	(Stylish/detailed/sensitive)	(Relevant/clear)
	Very good	Satisfactory

SQA 2011

Here is another reminder of the writing process:

Your proposals – your ideas for the piece of writing.

An outline plan – which shows the structure of your writing.

A first draft – your teacher will give you feedback on this.

A second draft – to be submitted to the SQA.

How to produce an effective piece of writing

Now let's look at how you might produce two pieces of writing for the portfolio: a personal/reflective essay (creative) and an argumentative essay (discursive).

Reflective writing

In reflective writing, it's vital to show that you are not just describing a personal experience, but also **reflecting** on that experience. Reflection might involve looking back on an event and trying to make sense of it, or thinking about what something means to you. Remember to write about your thoughts and feelings. If possible, try to avoid subjects that examiners will have seen many times before, e.g. the death of a grandparent or moving from primary to secondary school. Ask your teacher/tutor for advice if you are in any doubt.

Let's consider a reflective essay on a hobby or sport you enjoy. Here is a possible structure that you could take and adapt for a wide variety of reflective pieces. You can use this structure to write about any activity that means a lot to you.

Paragraph 1	Say what it is you like about the activity.
Paragraph 2	Shift the focus to consider the activity in a wider context.
Paragraph 3	Consider what other people think of you doing this activity.
Paragraph 4	Compare your experience to that of others.
Paragraph 5	Return to a detailed description of an aspect of the activity.
Paragraph 6	Describe how the activity has changed your life.

Now here is an example of that structure with some starter sentences for each paragraph.

Riding goofy – what snowboarding means to me

Paragraph 1

Say what it is you like about the activity – think about this (reflect) as you describe getting your gear ready for a day on the slopes. Describe what your first run feels like and reflect on your feelings of excitement. Describe what it feels like to complete a challenging descent or pull off a new trick. Start like this:

It's still dark as I get into the car and head for the Lecht. Most people are still in bed but getting up isn't difficult for me when I'm about to spend the day doing what I love best – snowboarding with my friends.

Paragraph 2

Now shift the focus from your own experience to consider snowboarding in a wider context. You might begin this paragraph with:

Other people might wonder what the point of my sport is. They don't understand that what they get at a football match or by playing on their Xbox or from buying that pair of shoes, I get from being on my board.

Paragraph 3

Consider what other people think of you doing this activity. You might begin:

To be honest, I know my mum is terrified every time she watches me trying out a new trick.

Paragraph 4

Compare your experience to that of others.

Shaun Whyte, the best snowboarder on the planet, says 'It's about pushing yourself to try new things and do the unexpected. Finally, and most importantly, it's about being creative.' I know exactly what he means.

Paragraph 5

Return to a description of the activity.

I take the chairlift to the top of the mountain. I feel anticipation, excitement and, yes, even a little fear. A blanket of white covers the slopes.

Paragraph 6

Describe how the activity has changed your life.

Confidence. Friendship. Challenge. These are the things that snowboarding has given me.

Once you have written your personal/reflective piece, use the following checklist to see if it includes all the important features:

Appropriate feature/technique	Included ✓
Captures the reader's interest (look again at your opening paragraph)	
Deals with a single idea/insight/experience	
Includes thoughts and feelings	
Uses a personal tone – the writing might be chatty, confidential, friendly, fairly informal etc.	
Gives a real sense of your personality	
States what you have learned or gained	
Shows the difference between how the experience or event was viewed **then** and how it is viewed **now** (if appropriate)	
Certain words are chosen to create particular effects	
Uses a variety of sentence structures (long sentences, short sentences, minor sentences, repetition, exclamation, ellipsis etc.) to create particular effects	
Uses imagery (simile, metaphor, personification) to create particular effects	
Consistently accurate spelling	
Consistently accurate sentence construction and punctuation	
Appropriate paragraphing	

Argumentative writing

In this kind of writing you have to consider at least **two** sides of an argument on a particular topic. The most straightforward structure to adopt is first to consider the **pros** (the arguments for), and then to consider the **cons** (the arguments against), before finally coming to a conclusion. This simple structure has the great advantage of keeping your line of thought clear for the reader:

- Introduction
- First argument for
- Second argument for
- Third argument for
- First argument against
- Second argument against
- Third argument against
- Conclusion

Of course you can add paragraphs if you have more points to make. You could also structure an argumentative essay like this:

- Introduction
- First point – arguments for
- First point – arguments against
- Second point – arguments for
- Second point – arguments against
- Third point – arguments for
- Third point – arguments against
- Conclusion

Whichever structure you choose, make sure you have planned your essay carefully before you start to write.

Let's consider an argumentative essay on the use of smartphones in the classroom. Here is a possible structure, some appropriate techniques to use and starter sentences for each paragraph.

> **EXAM TIP**
>
> Choose a topic that means something to you – you will almost always produce a better piece of writing as a result. For example, you may have looked at gun crime in America in your Modern Studies class but, unless that's something you're genuinely interested in, don't use it as a topic for your N5 English portfolio. A local issue such as, e.g. looking at the arguments for and against building new houses in a woodland near where you live, often works very well.

Smartphones in classrooms

Paragraph 1

Introduce the topic. Notice the use of questions to involve the reader.

The use of smartphones in classrooms has become a contentious issue in schools in recent months. Most pupils carry one of these miniature computers these days, and you can see them being used on the way to school, on the way home from school and in school social areas. Should we now allow these devices to be used in classrooms? Or are there too many dangers associated with them?

Paragraph 2

Make the first argument *for*.

One argument in favour of using smartphones in the classroom is that pupils can use them to make a note of any homework given out. This means that we can do away with bulky paper planners and homework diaries.

Paragraph 3

Make the second argument *for*. Always try to link the sections or paragraphs in your writing effectively.

As well as this, smartphones can also be used as calculators in maths and science.

Paragraph 4

Make the third argument *for*. Notice the use of evidence.

In addition to these uses, the best thing about a smartphone is that it lets you access the internet. You can research information for your subjects online or download materials from your school website. You no longer have to go to a school computer suite to do this – you can do all these things in class. Last year, a study in Manchester showed that pupils improved their test scores by 15% if they were allowed access to smartphones in class.

Paragraph 5

Now make a final argument *for*.

Furthermore, since school is supposed to prepare pupils for the world of work where smartphones are in use all the time, it seems only right that pupils learn to work with these devices in school.

Paragraph 6

Now discuss the *cons* – the arguments *against*. Make your first point.

Despite all these positives, there are also dangers in allowing pupils to use smartphones in class. The first one to consider is that films of teachers and pupils might end up being posted on the internet without their knowledge.

Paragraph 7

Make the second argument *against*.

Secondly, there is the argument that pupils might be distracted by social media apps and messages received during a lesson.

Paragraph 8

Now consider your final argument *against*.

Finally, what do schools do for pupils who do not have a smartphone?

Paragraph 9

Now make your conclusion.

It is clear that there are some convincing arguments against having smartphones in the classroom. It is also clear, however, that schools need to keep up with new technology and that the advantages of using smartphones in class outweigh the disadvantages.

Don't forget to acknowledge any sources (print, digital, TV or film) you have consulted. You can simply list these at the end of your writing, e.g.

http://www.bbc.co.uk/news/education-43386670

http://www.bbc.co.uk/news/education-21476385

Once you have written your argumentative piece, use the following checklist to see if it includes all the important features:

Appropriate feature/technique	Included ✓
Clear introduction	
Clear, logical structure (paragraphing, topic sentences)	
Effective links between sections/arguments/paragraphs	
Effective use of vocabulary to signal shifts in arguments ('however', 'furthermore', 'in addition to this', 'despite this …')	
Appropriate tone (suggested by word choice and other language features)	
Use of comparisons to illustrate a point ('Telling a pupil to give up their smartphone would be like …')	
Arguments supported by evidence (statistics etc.)	
Arguments challenged by evidence (statistics etc.)	
Uses a variety of sentence structures (long sentences, short sentences, minor sentences, repetition, list, exclamation, ellipsis etc.) to create particular effects	
Consistently accurate spelling	
Consistently accurate sentence construction and punctuation	
Sources consulted are listed at the end	
More than one source has been used	
Sources used are credible, up to date and relevant	

EXAM TIP

In this kind of writing, remember to make use of the techniques you've learned about in your work for the **Reading for understanding, analysis and evaluation** paper.

Ideas for creative writing

Personal/reflective

- Why snowboarding is important to me
- What my team means to me
- Sibling rivalry
- The animals in my life
- A narrow escape – and what it taught me
- A keepsake that means a lot to me
- What I've gained from performing in front of others
- Living in Scotland today
- My family
- Friends
- The passing of time
- Challenges I have faced
- The important things in life are …
- Solitude

Prose fiction

Titles

- Trapped!
- The waiting game
- Star
- An appointment with death
- Speed
- The magic box
- The network
- Playing with fire

Starters

- Kirsty walked into the office. Silence. She hadn't expected this …
- It is a truth universally acknowledged that a Scotsman in possession of a carry out must be in want of a party.
- Fifty clicks still to go and only enough fuel for 20. Commander Grant looked round at his ragtag army …
- I rang the bell. No response. I rang it again. Still nothing. I rang it for a third time. From somewhere deep inside that old house I heard someone *or something* begin to move.
- Fiona looked at the faces around the table. 'I'm not sure I even know these people any more,' she thought to herself.

Poetry

Anything is a potential subject for a poem. Why not choose a particular verse form to express your ideas? Perhaps a sonnet or a villanelle?

A dramatic script (possible scenarios)

- Two friends fall out on their way home from school
- A game of cards (who might the players be?)
- A young person visiting an elderly relative in a care home
- Three people waiting to be interviewed for a job
- A courtroom scene
- Two people on a first date
- An unexpected guest interrupts a family celebration
- A psychiatrist and a patient
- A son or daughter having to apologise to their parents for some misdemeanour
- A corner shop and its eccentric owner
- A dramatic monologue from the point of view of a small child
- Three people stuck in a lift

Discursive writing

- A transactional essay giving information on the discipline system used in your school
- An argumentative essay that explores the topic of social media
- A persuasive essay on why all pupils should use smartphones in class
- A report on the time allocated to PE in Scottish schools
- A persuasive essay on what needs to be done to improve Scottish football
- An argumentative essay on whether Scotland is a truly multicultural society
- A persuasive essay on why you shouldn't go to university
- An argumentative essay on single-sex schools
- A report on the different languages used in Scotland today
- An argumentative piece on Scottish independence
- A persuasive essay on the benefits of renewable energy
- An argumentative essay on the influence of religion on our lives

Understanding, analysis and evaluation questions

First let's look at an example of the sort of passage and questions that you will have to deal with in the SQA examination. We'll start by looking at the first element of the question paper. This consists of a passage (always non-fiction) and around eight or nine questions.

Remember that the questions are designed to test your understanding, analysis and evaluation of the passage.

- **Understanding** questions ask you to show your knowledge of **what** the writer is telling the reader.
- **Analysis** questions ask you to look at **how** the writer gets their message across.
- **Evaluation** questions ask you to decide **how effective** the writer's use of language is.

You can expect to be asked to **summarise** parts of the passage and to make **inferences** from its content. We'll look at both of these types of questions below.

Pay particular attention to 'command words' in the questions. The SQA provides the following information:

The following main command words are generally used in this question paper:

- **explain** (why): used to assess understanding of a writer's ideas (always followed by 'in your own words')
- **explain** (how): used to assess the skills of analysis
- **identify:** used to assess the skill of summarising (identifying the main points or ideas)[3]

Here are some examples of these command words used in the 2017 SQA exam paper:

The writer tells us that 'football is a beautiful meritocracy' (line 36). **Explain in your own words** three points the writer makes about merit being rewarded in the rest of this paragraph.

Look at lines 1–7, and **explain how** one example of the writer's word choice makes it clear that his memories of childhood football are positive.

Look at lines 12–25, and **identify in your own words** six points which the writer makes about young people hoping to become professional footballers.

_____

[3]National 5 English Course Specification, SQA

Types of questions

Own words

Questions that ask you to answer 'in your own words' or 'in your own words as far as possible' are usually testing two things.

1. Can you find the relevant evidence in the passage?

2. Your vocabulary.

When answering 'own words' questions, you might find it useful to think of this process as **locate** and **translate**. You need to **locate** the answer and then **translate** it into your own words.

Let's look at an example of this in action. Read the following extract from an article about an online celebrity, Poppy:

> Poppy says Poppy is an alien, an object, a computer, your pet. But Poppy is a character portrayed by the musician Moriah Poppy, born Moriah Pereira, created with the director Titanic Sinclair, born Corey Mixter, both of Los Angeles. She is a pop singer, soon to be the star of her own TV show. She is the sort of celebrity who could not have existed even half a decade ago: born of and beloved by the internet, and essentially unknown outside of it.
>
> Elle Hunt, *The Guardian*, 11 December 2017

Now imagine that you were asked the following question:

Explain **in your own words three** points the writer makes about what 'sort of celebrity' Poppy is?

The first thing you would do is **locate** the answer. It's a good idea to get into the habit of highlighting or underlining words in the passage.

Poppy says Poppy is an alien, an object, a computer, your pet. But Poppy is a character portrayed by the musician Moriah Poppy, born Moriah Pereira, created with the director Titanic Sinclair, born Corey Mixter, both of Los Angeles. She is a pop singer, soon to be the star of her own TV show. She is the sort of celebrity who could not have existed even half a decade ago: born of and beloved by the internet, and essentially unknown outside of it.

Now that you've **located** the answer you have to **translate** it into your own words. This is where the test of your vocabulary comes in.

Instead of

'could not have existed half a decade ago'

you could say

'it's only recently someone like her has even been possible'.

Instead of

'born of and beloved by the internet'

you could say

'created and adored online'.

Instead of

'essentially unknown outside of it'

you could say

'her fame is limited to the digital world'.

In the exam you could write your answer in sentences or just use bullet points:

- it's only recently someone like her has even been possible
- created and adored online
- her fame is limited to the digital world

You might also be asked to summarise or identify a number of key points from a longer section of the text.

Look at this question, which was part of the SQA 2017 N5 Reading for understanding, analysis and evaluation paper:

Look at lines 12–25, and identify **in your own words six** points which the writer makes about young people hoping to become professional footballers.	6

You can see that this is worth 6 marks – that's a lot of marks for one question (20% of the total marks in this paper) so it's important to approach the question in the right way. As we saw above, you should locate the relevant parts of the text, highlight or underline them (it might also help to number them) and then turn them into your own words in a bullet point list.

It has been reported that 98 per cent of those signed by English teams at 16 fail[1] to make the transition into professional football. Many struggle to cope with rejection[2] at such a tender age. Clinical psychologists report that many suffer anxiety, a loss of confidence and, in some cases, depression. These youngsters are often described as being 'left on football's scrapheap'.[3]

It seems to me, though, that the number rejected is, in fact, far higher. After all, the sifting process starts from the first time you kick a ball[4] at the local park. I was one of the few who made it into my school team (I captained it). But when I went to trial for the district team, surrounded by the best players from all the schools in the area, the standard was high. Parents were everywhere. I remember my heart beating out of my chest when the 'scouts' arrived.[5] I did not make it. I was crushed by the disappointment. How could it be otherwise? But I also realised that the race had only just started for those who had made the cut. Of those who made it into the district team, only a handful were picked by Reading, the local club.[6] And of those who made it to Reading, only a fraction made it into professional football. Perhaps none made it all the way to the top flight.

SQA 2017 Matthew Syed, *The Times*

- the vast majority do not succeed
- lots of them find it hard to accept being told they're not good enough
- the process is heartless – they are treated like useless objects
- deciding who makes it starts very early
- being assessed causes them to be nervous
- even if they enjoy some initial success that doesn't mean they make it all the way

If you are asked to consider more than one paragraph in a passage, it's a good idea to look first at the **topic sentence** of each paragraph – the sentence that gives the clearest idea of what the paragraph is about. This is often (but not always) the first sentence in each paragraph. Remember that you are looking for only the most important details.

Read the passage on pages 38–39, 'The men behind the morphsuit', and see if you can summarise it in no more than **seven** bullet points.

Check your answers online at www.leckieandleckie.co.uk.

The men behind the morphsuit

It started out as a hilarious prank at a stag-do and has morphed into a million-pound fancy-dress phenomenon. Tom Lamont meets the three Scotsmen who have given the world the mighty morphsuit.

Shape of things to come: revellers cover up in a selection of morphsuits at the T in the Park festival in Kinross. Photograph: Ross Gilmore for the Observer

Not long ago, three friends from Scotland went out for drinks wearing brightly coloured costumes from Japan. It would prove a pivotal night of fancy dress.

5 The trio – brothers Ali and Fraser Smeaton, and their friend from Edinburgh University, Gregor Lawson – were skiing in Canada. They decided to hit the local bars wearing 'zentai suits' – skin-tight Japanese leotards that covered them from head to toe. It was an idea Gregor had pinched from a stag weekend, where one of the attendees, newly back from Asia, had shown up in a vivid blue zentai. 'Everyone wanted to
10 buy him a drink,' recalls Gregor. 'I'd never seen anything like it.'

In Canada, dressed up in zentai suits of their own, the trio were likewise admired. 'The resort shut down, people were stopping us in the street,' says Ali Smeaton. The friends wondered if they'd stumbled on a way to make some cash – perhaps fund next year's ski trip. 'A bit
15 of pocket money,' says Ali. 'We'd take something that existed, give it a name, change certain physical elements, bring it to the masses.' One modification they decided on right away was that their version would be made of something more see-through. They'd been walking around virtually blind.

20   That was in early 2009. Today, the morphsuit (as the trio boozily agreed to name their product) is a multimillion-pound concern. A zip-up costume made of polyester and Lycra, all-enveloping so that the wearer looks like a featureless mannequin, the morphsuit has become commonplace at sporting events and stag nights, festivals and parties.

25   It has also made unusual incursions into the world beyond. The day after bin Laden was killed, in 2011, Al Jazeera carried a photograph of an anonymous American celebrating outside the White House in a morphsuit patterned with stars and stripes.

      The Smeatons and Gregor hear of barely credible use of their creation
30   almost every day. In the first week of July there were morphsuits spotted at the European Championships in Kiev (where three Italian football fans in the red, white and green of *il tricolore* watched their team lose) and at the Olympic torch relay in Warwick (a lone man in an all-body union flag watching the flame pass). Police in
35   Gloucestershire warned of a man acting suspiciously in a morphsuit in the Forest of Dean. At the same time, Ali, Fraser and Gregor – now in their early 30s, together known as AFG Media – made national news when they secured £4.2m in funding to expand their business. It already had a projected annual turnover of £11m.

                            Tom Lamont, *The Observer*, 5 August 2012

EXAM TIP

This is an easy skill to practise. You can take virtually any newspaper article in print or online and identify the main points within it. Try to do this regularly (once or twice a week) with articles from quality newspapers.

Questions that ask you to infer things

As well as identifying key facts in the passage, you might sometimes be asked to **infer** things.

Look at this question, which was part of the SQA 2016 N5 Reading for understanding, analysis and evaluation paper:

Throughout the passage, we are given information and clues about Idina Menzel's personality. **Using your own words** as far as possible, identify **five** things that we learn about her personality from the passage.	5

The word 'clues' is crucial here. Being able to infer something means working it out without actually being told it. It's all about looking for clues and then using them to arrive at the answer.

For example, if you walk into someone's house for the first time and in the hallway you see a bowl filled with dog food and a dog's lead hanging up, then it would be reasonable to infer that the person you are visiting owns a dog.

Here is an extract from the script of the BBC TV drama series *Sherlock*. Look at how Sherlock Holmes is able to infer things about Dr Watson from their first meeting.

Sherlock Holmes:	I'm a consulting detective. Only one in the world. I invented the job.
Watson:	What does that mean?
Sherlock Holmes:	It means when the police are out of their depth, which is always, they consult me.
Watson:	The police don't consult amateurs.
Sherlock Holmes:	When I met you for the first time yesterday, I said Afghanistan or Iraq. You looked surprised.
Watson:	Yes, how did you know?
Sherlock Holmes:	I didn't know, I saw. Your haircut, the way you hold yourself says military. And your conversation as you entered the room …
Watson:	A bit different from my day.
Sherlock Holmes:	… said trained at Barts – so army doctor. Obvious. Your face is tanned but no tan above the wrists. You've been abroad, but not sunbathing. Your limp's really bad when you walk, but you don't ask for a chair when you stand. Like you've forgotten about it, so it's at least partly psychosomatic. That says the original circumstances of the injury were traumatic. Wounded in action, suntan – Afghanistan or Iraq.
Watson:	You said I had a therapist.

Sherlock Holmes:	You've got a psychosomatic limp, of course you've got a therapist. Then there's your brother. Your phone. It's expensive, email enabled, MP3 player. You're looking for a flatshare. You wouldn't waste money on this – it's a gift then. Scratches. Not one, many over time. It's been in the same pocket as keys and coins. The man sitting next to me wouldn't treat his one luxury item like this. So it's had a previous owner. Next bit's easy. You know it already.
	'Harry Watson – from Clara x x x'
Watson:	The engraving?
Sherlock Holmes:	Harry Watson – clearly a family member who's given you his old phone. Not your father – this is a young man's gadget. Could be a cousin, but you're a war hero who can't find a place to live. Unlikely you've got an extended family, certainly not one you're close to, so brother it is. Now, Clara – who's Clara? Three kisses says it's a romantic attachment. Expensive phone says wife, not girlfriend. Must've given it to him recently – this model's only six months old. Marriage in trouble then – six months on, and already he's given it away? If she'd left *him*, he would have kept it. People do, sentiment. But no, he wanted rid of it – he left *her*. He gave the phone to you, that says he wants you to stay in touch. You're looking for cheap accommodation and you're not going to your brother for help? That says you've got problems with him. Maybe you liked his wife, maybe you don't like his drinking.
Watson:	How can you possibly know about the drinking?
Sherlock Holmes:	Shot in the dark. Good one, though. Power connection – tiny little scuff marks round the edge. Every night he goes to plug it in and charge but his hands are shaking. You never see those marks on a sober man's phone, never see a drunk's without them.

Sherlock, 'A Study in Pink', Hartswood Films/Steven Moffat

Being able to infer things when you are reading involves you making use of the clues in the text – just like Sherlock Holmes does.

Read the passage on pages 42–43, 'Going to Sea in a Sieve', carefully and, just like Sherlock Holmes, see if you can **infer** the answers to the questions that follow. Make a note of the **clues** you use to make your deductions. Check your answers online at www.leckieandleckie.co.uk.

I am seven years old and the car in which I sit is, by now, totally enveloped in flames. The old banger had had a good run. Ever since we had found it abandoned on our dump – in the 1960s, bombsites were called 'dumps' – we had been using it as a kind of base camp.
5 Now, with its slashed front seats exposing clumps of horse-hair, together with the plywood tea chests we had squeezed into the rear after the seats were removed, it seemed to almost beg for a playful match. So we had all piled in, popped a Swan Vesta and declared whoever got out first was a coward and whoever stayed till last was
10 the game's winner. I know, I know. And kids these days make all that fuss about Nintendo.

On fire for about ten minutes now, it was clearly no longer a matter of when I should get out but whether I could get out. But I wasn't moving. Not yet. Not me.

15 The tea chest in which I squatted was starting to give off thin wisps of smoke that foretold, any second now, it would probably go up in a huge fireball. Still I was determined to win. Besides, other than me, there was only Pete left inside this blazing wreck and Kingy was certainly no champion when it came to a rattling good game
20 of chicken like this. He would definitely lose his nerve before long – I mean, I had to believe that or what was the point of the whole exercise?

We looked at each other defiantly, head and shoulders poking up above the tin-lined edges of our tea chests, the flames now billowing
25 along the roof of the rusted old vehicle, the smoke funnelling out through where once had been doors on the doomed Ford Popular. The thick plume billowed across the bombsite.

> The front of the car had predictably gone up like a gasworks, disqualifying Tommy Hodges, Stephen Micalef and Tony Plumpton
> 30　almost immediately as they panicked and leapt out, it seemed to me, prematurely. They hadn't lasted ten seconds. Now it was down to just Kingy and me. And though I daren't show it, yes I was beginning to find the growing inferno's repeated metallic bangs, pops and fizzes a tad alarming. But did he?
>
> 35　Of course what neither I nor Kingy, nor any of our half-dozen or so friends cheering us on from the relative safety of three feet away, had entertained for a moment was the idea that there might still be a petrol tank lurking within the old banger.
>
> And it was growing fearsomely hot in there …
>
> 　　　　　　　　　　　　　　　Danny Baker, *Going to Sea in a Sieve*

	Clues	Answer
1. Where is this passage set?		
2. Who do you think 'we' are?		
3. What is a Swan Vesta?		
4. Why is Pete referred to as Kingy?		
5. What is a Ford Popular?		
6. From what sort of text is this passage taken?		

Look back at the SQA question at the start of this section where you are asked to **infer** five things about Idina Menzel's personality. The following sentence is part of the passage:

When *Let It Go* was nominated for Best Song at the Oscars a year ago, it was Cara (her sister) whom Menzel took as her date.

From this you could infer that

- Idina has a close relationship with her sister and that would be one of the five things required in the bag.

Language techniques

In the **Reading for understanding, analysis and evaluation** paper you will be asked questions about the writer's use of language. A question might ask about 'the writer's language' or 'language features' or specific techniques such as word choice or sentence structure. Here are three typical questions:

Explain fully why the simile 'like tiny stars in a galaxy' is effective here.	2

Look at lines 42–47. By referring to **two** language features, explain how the writer makes clear her view about drugs. You should refer to **two different** language features such as word choice, imagery or sentence structure.	4

Look at lines 15–18, and explain how **two** features of the writer's sentence structure are used to highlight important points.	4

Make sure you pay close attention to what it is you are being asked to do. If the question refers to specific features then **only refer to those features** in your answer; if the question refers to language features in general and doesn't refer to specific features, then you can choose to deal with any of the following:

- word choice
- imagery
- sentence structure
- punctuation
- sound
- tone

or, in fact, *any* language technique you can spot the writer using.

In your answers to these kinds of questions, you will always get 1 mark for quoting or referring to a particular example of a language feature and 1 mark for commenting on its effect.

Word choice questions

Questions on word choice are usually very straightforward to answer. All you need to do is **quote** an example of the writer's word choice (usually a single word or phrase) and then **say what it suggests**. Think about the connotations of the word – the ideas associated with that word.

Here is another example from the SQA 2017 paper:

Look at lines 1–7, and explain how **one** example of the writer's word choice makes it clear that his memories of childhood football are positive.	2

Your answer should look like this:

'endlessly' suggests his enjoyment seemed never to stop.

You would get one mark for quoting the word 'endlessly' and one mark for the comment that follows. That is all you need to write – you don't need to rewrite the question or answer in a great long sentence.

Sentence structure

Questions on sentence structure are also very straightforward to answer. All you need to do is **quote** an example of a technique or feature and then provide a relevant comment.

You should be able to identify the following language features:

- **list** – look for sequences of single words or longer expressions
- **minor sentence** – an incomplete sentence (a sentence without a finite verb)
- **short sentence** – often used for impact or emphasis
- **repetition** – look for repeated words, expressions or structures
- **climax** – words or expressions building to a high point
- **anti-climax** – the writer seems to be building to a high point but adds something to deliberately weaken the effect, often to create a comic effect
- **rhetorical question** – a question asked to create an effect rather than to seek information
- **parenthesis** – extra information inserted into a sentence
- **inversion** – where the usual word order of a sentence is turned around to highlight particular words or expressions
- **juxtaposition** – where words are placed together to achieve a particular effect (when two words of *opposite* meaning are placed together you get an oxymoron, e.g. bitter sweet; old news)
- **punctuation** (including comma, colon, semi-colon, inverted commas etc.) – see the following table:

Punctuation	Use	Examples
Comma ,	To separate items in a list	Russia, Germany, France and Italy are all significant players on the world stage.
	To mark parenthesis	The dancers, all under twenty-five, ignored the onlooker.
	To separate clauses in a sentence	That night I tried oysters for the first time, which turned out to be a bad decision.

Colon :	To introduce a quotation	The school motto remains burned in my memory: 'Sic itur ad astra – This is the way to the stars!'
	To introduce a list	Memories flooded back: the meal; the film; the walk home and the painful goodbye.
	To introduce an explanation or expansion	The Scots were unlucky: two shots hit the bar.
Semi-colon ;	To separate statements that are closely connected or to act as a 'hinge' in a balanced sentence	The dollar increased in value; the pound fell.
	To separate longer expressions in a list	All the ingredients for a successful study session were in place: a quiet room; revision materials to hand; healthy snacks; appropriate music.
Single dash –	To highlight what follows by separating it from the rest of the sentence	Up ahead of them was their greatest challenge – the steepest rock of the climb.
	To add an afterthought	She was the most popular girl in the class – at least that's what she believed.
Paired dash – – or Brackets ( )	To indicate extra information within a sentence (parenthesis)	The exam – National 5 History – was harder than expected.
Inverted commas ' ... '	To mark direct speech	'Are you sure?' she asked.
	To indicate titles	'Bold Girls' is one of the Scottish texts for National 5 English.
	To suggest words are being used in a particular way, e.g. to suggest irony	The police 'assisted' the troublesome fan away from the ground.
Question mark ?	To indicate a question	Why do we make pupils sit exams?
Exclamation mark !	To indicate surprise, shock or someone shouting in direct speech	'Come on Scotland!' she yelled.
	To mark an exclamation	The class continued to behave badly – and that was after the head teacher had been in to see them!
Ellipsis ...	To indicate missing words in a sentence	'We could go to the ...'
	To indicate where a speaker breaks off without completing a sentence	The sheer number of apps available on your phone: Twitter, Facebook ...
	To suggest a list could be continued	Instagram, Snapchat ... means that there are more and more ways to avoid real work.

Other language features you might be expected to recognise and comment on include:

- **Hyperbole or exaggeration** – a common feature of persuasive writing
- **Contrast** – always make sure you refer to both sides of the contrast

So to answer a question like this one:

Look at lines 43–46, and explain how **one** feature of the writer's sentence structure is used to highlight an important point.	2

your answer should look like this:

repetition of 'a new' emphasises the possibility of a fresh start

You would get 1 mark for identifying the use of the technique or feature (in this case, repetition) and 1 mark for the comment that follows.

In your comment you should always refer to the **effect** the use of the technique has.

Link questions

Another fairly common type of question in the **Reading for understanding, analysis and evaluation** paper is the 'link' question. It usually looks something like this:

By referring to the sentence in lines 54–55, explain how it helps to provide a link between the writer's ideas at this point in the passage.	2

In order to answer this question it might help to think of the sentence as a link in a chain.

A link in a chain is attached to the link that comes before it and to the link that comes after it. Your task is to find the bit of the sentence that is 'attached' or refers back to an idea from earlier in the passage. You then quote those words and add a comment about what they refer back to. Alternatively, you can find the bit of the sentence that is attached to or introduces an idea that comes later in the passage. You then quote those words and add a comment about what they introduce.

Let's look at an example. Here is an extract from *Sapiens – A Brief History of Humankind* by Yuval Noah Harari. In it, he discusses the development of writing.

> The Mesopotamians eventually started to want to write down things other than monotonous mathematical data. Between 3000 BC and 2500 BC more and more signs were added to the Sumerian system, gradually transforming it
> 5   into a full script that we today call cuneiform. By 2500 BC, kings were using cuneiform to issue decrees, priests were using it to record oracles, and less exalted citizens were using it to write personal letters. At roughly the same time, Egyptians developed another full script known as
> 10   hieroglyphics. Other full scripts were developed in China around 1200 BC and in Central America around 1000–500 BC.
>
> From these initial centres, full scripts spread far and wide, taking on various new forms and novel tasks. People began to write poetry, history books, romances, dramas,
> 15   prophecies and cook books. Yet writing's most important task continued to be the storage of reams of mathematical data, and that task remained the prerogative of partial script.

If you were asked this question:

By referring to the sentence in lines 12–13, explain how it helps to provide a link between the writer's ideas at this point in the passage.	2

you could answer as follows:

'these initial centres' refers back to the places mentioned in the previous paragraph where writing systems first started to appear.

Or you could say:

'various new forms' introduces the idea of the many new genres of writing which the writer goes on to list later on in this paragraph.

Either answer would get the full 2 marks on offer, 1 for the quotation and 1 for the comment.

EXAM TIP

Look out for words such as 'this' or 'these', which might help you identify the words that refer back to a previous idea.

Look out for words such as 'yet', 'but' or 'however', which might also signal a turning point in the writer's argument.

The effectiveness of a paragraph

You might find that a question asks you about the effectiveness of a particular paragraph – perhaps as an introduction or as a conclusion to the passage. You might be asked to identify ideas and techniques the writer uses or you might be asked to choose any example of the writer's language and say why it is effective.

Always begin with a comment on the effectiveness. Make some kind of evaluative judgement about how successful the writer has been in getting their points across. It's usually easier to be positive than negative. Start like this:

The final paragraph is very effective because . . .

Then deal with ideas and language.

Ideas

Some things to consider:

- Does the paragraph sum up some of the points made earlier in the passage?
- Does it refer to anything from the opening of the passage (a common technique that gives a nice sense of 'circularity' in the structure of the article)?
- Does it include a clear statement of the writer's opinion?
- Does it try to involve the reader or address the reader directly?

Language

Identify techniques as you would for questions elsewhere in the passage, e.g.

- sentence structure
- word choice
- imagery
- sound
- tone
- punctuation

and comment on how they help to reinforce the effectiveness of the paragraph.

Here is an example of what an answer to a question on the effectiveness of a paragraph might look like.

The final paragraph is effective because it sums up the writer's arguments about dangerous sports. It is clear she disapproves of them. The short, blunt sentence 'They're just bonkers' makes it clear what she thinks about BASE jumpers. 'falling into oblivion' refers back to the description of the jump in the opening paragraph.

If you are asked about the opening paragraph, then the same principles apply – except you should look at how the paragraph **introduces** the ideas in the passage or **captures** the reader's attention.

Other language features

- Sound

Look out for examples of alliteration, onomatopoeia, sibilance.

- Tone

It's easy to identify someone's tone of voice when that person is speaking to you. For example you can usually tell if they are being serious about something or not.

Identifying tone in a passage on the page is more challenging. It's a good idea to think of tone as the writer's attitude to what they are writing about. Some of the more obvious tones a writer might employ are:

- serious
- humorous
- ironic
- sarcastic
- light-hearted

- formal
- informal
- angry
- frustrated

But this list is not exhaustive – there are, in fact, a huge range of possible tones you might encounter.

If you are asked a specific question about tone or want to refer to it when asked about language features in general, then follow the same pattern of answer that we've looked at above: **quote** an example of a particular feature and then add a **comment** about how it contributes to the tone the writer is using. Typical answers to questions about tone might look like this:

The word 'despicable' helps to indicate the angry tone adopted by the writer as it is a much stronger word than just 'bad'.

The use of inverted commas around 'enjoyed' suggests the writer is being rather sarcastic about the value of the experience.

Now that you have looked at the sorts of questions that you might be asked and the range of language features you need to know about, let's have a look at an exam-type passage and a set of questions. The article is taken from *Time* magazine and is typical of the type of passage you can expect to encounter in the exam in terms of its level of difficulty.

Read the passage and then look at the questions and the accompanying suggestions about how to answer them.

Fortnite

Fortnite, a video game released without much fanfare last July, is now arguably the most popular diversion in the world; a cultural

5   juggernaut on a par with *Star Wars*, or *Minecraft* – though one now also attracting players with a $100m prize fund. Playgrounds jostle as children showboat dance moves

10 copied from the game, while parents tip from mournful anxiety about screentime quotas, to blessed relief that here is a game that encourages teamwork, compromise

15 and communication between their otherwise monosyllabic adolescents.

Fortnite borrows the premise of the Japanese novel *Battle Royale* and *The Hunger Games*, in which contestants are sent to an island where they must scavenge and fight until only one remains. In *Fortnite* you are dropped along with 99 other players from a flying bus, and

20 parachute on to a candy-coloured island. Every few minutes a lethal electrical storm draws closer, herding survivors toward a final standoff.

As in life, character is destiny: the meek will cower in a bush as those around them pick each other off, before furtively scurrying from hut to hillock. The bolshie will fly directly to the most populated towns and

25 engage in thrilling races to be the first to find a gun and a pocketful of bullets. The homemaker will harvest wood from trees and build a base, sometimes into the clouds, from where they can peek, snipe and fend off invaders. Over the 20 minutes that each game lasts, 100 small stories of bravery and cowardice, skill and haplessness accumulate

30 and intersect. Matches are equal parts exhilarating, unexpected and, for all but the victor, usually indescribably maddening.

While *Fortnite's* style and rhythm are unique, the template is not. It closely follows *PlayerUnknown's Battlegrounds* (PUBG), a game that dominated the PC game charts last year. In September, its producer

35 Chang Han Kim stated that his studio was "concerned" about *Fortnite's* similarities, and that his team intended to explore legal action. By March, however, there was only legal inaction, and *Fortnite* had, among the world's children at least, overtaken Battlegrounds as the game of the moment.

40   This success is due to a variety of factors. For one, Epic Games is one of the industry's oldest outfits, experienced in building and maintaining online competitive video games since the dawn of the internet. While PUBG's updates have been slow and unexciting, *Fortnite's* updates launch with military-grade regularity and have introduced a flurry

45   of new items and wild, one-off game modes (50 v 50, Sniper rifles only). The game's aesthetic, which is bright, colourful and decidedly un-bloody, has helped convince parents that this is a world of harmless, cartoonish violence. PUBG, by contrast, is brown and gory.

    Then in March the musician Drake, the rapper Travis Scott and the

50   American football player JuJu Smith-Schuster joined professional video game streamer Tyler "Ninja" Blevins in a *Fortnite* squad. Footage of their play session, broadcast on the live-streaming service Twitch, broke the record for the most-viewed episode on the internet. The *Washington* Post reported that at one point more than 630,000

55   viewers were logged on to the match, which also trended on Twitter.

    In America, where the word "fortnight" is not in usage, unsavvy social media users started posting about a new phenomenon called "fork knife" (a term then adopted, titteringly, by some players). In playgrounds, word of the game has spread virally, not only through

60   excited recaps of the previous night's matches, but also, extraordinarily, via the Floss, a dance move that originated on YouTube in 2014 but was popularised by *Fortnite*. (The game allows players to aggressively perform a variety of dance moves at one another, either as a form of bonding or antagonism.)

65   *Fortnite's* business model is quietly revolutionary. The studio makes money not from point-of-sale (it's free to download) but from selling digital costumes, known as skins, to the players. Each day a new wardrobe is put up for sale on the game's storefront, for a few pounds apiece. Players can dress their digital avatar as a ninja, a medieval

70   knight, an Olympic skier, or a skeleton, to name but a few, and in this way stand out from the crowd. The men and women who design these costumes have become some of the most important members of *Fortnite's* development team: it is through their fashion work that the game makes its money.

75   This art of virtual costuming is rapidly changing the medium's business model. In 2015 the Los Angeles game developer Riot, one of the first companies to adopt the model, reputedly made almost $2bn from selling digital clothes for its game *League of Legends*. More developers are following suit as they seek to produce a game that

80   becomes a "service" to which players return each day, rather than a one-time experience like a film or TV box set. By offering their game for free, studios hope to quickly build an online community, which is

then monetised by digital fashion. Epic refused to comment on how many *Fortnite* outfits it has sold, stating only that as of February the

85 game had "more than 45 million players".

Now the game is poised to become a sport. While, in the early months, professional players, Twitch streamers and YouTubers ignored the game, viewing it as too childish for their audiences, that has now changed. Blevins is reportedly making $500,000 a month from streaming the

90 game, while daily videos posted by Ali-A, one of the most popular British YouTubers, routinely pass 2 million views in 24 hours.

Epic remains coy about figures, but the dramatic scale of the game's success was hinted at last Monday when the company announced a $100m prize pool for *Fortnite* tournaments over the next year. While

95 other developers rush to create their own *Battle Royales*, it seems increasingly likely that *Fortnite* will be the last man standing.

Questions

1.	(a) Look at lines 1–15. Identify **in your own words** as far as possible, **four** positive points the writer makes about *Fortnite*.	4
	This question tests your ability to find information and then tests your understanding and your vocabulary. Remember to locate and translate. Look at lines 1–15 and underline or highlight three points the writer makes. Number them as well if it helps. You should be able to locate the following in the passage:	
	1. "the most popular diversion in the world"	
	2. "on a par with *Star Wars*, or *Minecraft*"	
	3. "attracting players with a $100m prize fund"	
	4. "Playgrounds jostle as children showboat dance moves copied from the game"	
	5. "parents tip from mournful anxiety about screentime quotas, to blessed relief"	
	6. "a game that encourages teamwork, compromise and communication"	
	Now all you have to do is select four of them and translate them into your own words. You would get 1 mark for each one you get right. Let's say you pick 1, 3, 5 and 6. Four bullet points will do nicely. Your answer might look like this:	
	• It's the number one pastime on the planet	
	• You can win lots of money playing it	
	• Parents are not worried about their children playing it	
	• It makes its players work things out together and speak to each other	

	(b) Explain how **two** examples of the writer's language in these lines help to reinforce the idea of *Fortnite's* success.	**4**
	Quote + comment required here x 2. 1 mark for the quotation and 1 mark for the comment.	
	• the superlative "most popular diversion" emphasises the success of the game	
	• "juggernaut" suggests it's enormous and difficult to stop	
	• "attracting" suggests players are drawn to it	
	• "$100m prize fund" huge sum highlights the commercial investment going along with the game	
	• "jostle" suggests the buzz of activity caused by the game	
	• "children showboat dance moves" suggests the game has prompted children to perform	
	• "blessed relief" suggests a very welcome respite for parents	
	• the list/triad, "encourages teamwork, compromise and communication" emphasises the positive aspects of the game	
2.	Look at lines 22–31 ("As in life . . . maddening"). Explain how two examples of the writer's use of sentence structure makes it clear what a game of *Fortnite* is like.	**4**
	Remember this sort of question is often easier than you think. Find and quote/refer to an example of the writer's use of this feature (1 mark) and then add a comment to explain what it does (1 mark). Do this twice and you'll get the four marks. Look for obvious features such as lists, repetitions, triads, short sentences and particular features of punctuation. Your answer might look like any two of these:	
	The colon after "destiny" introduces an explanation of what "character is destiny" means – how different players will behave in the game.	
	or	
	The repeated structure of "the meek . . ."; "The bolshie . . ."; "The homemaker . . ." shows us the different player personalities.	
	or	
	The use of a list/triad "peek, snipe and fend off" illustrates typical actions in the game.	
	or	
	The pairs of opposite ideas "bravery and cowardice, skill and haplessness" show the contrasting events/actions in the game.	
	or	
	The triad "exhilarating, unexpected . . . maddening" sums up the exciting yet frustrating experience of playing the game.	

3.	By referring to the sentence in line 40 ("This success…"), explain how it helps to provide a link between the writer's ideas at this point in the passage.	2

Remember to identify the bits of the sentence that refer back and/or the bits that introduce what follows. If it helps, draw arrows on the passage. In this case you should see that:

- "This success" refers back to *Fortnite* becoming the most popular game in the world which is mentioned in the previous paragraph
- "due to a variety of factors" introduces the reasons behind its success that the writer outlines in lines 40–48

Either of these will do for your answer. You get 1 mark for the quote and 1 mark for saying what it refers back to or introduces. Again, you just have to supply the answer; there's no need to write out the words of the question or answer in long sentences.

"This success" refers back to Fortnite becoming the most popular game in the world which the writer told us about in the previous paragraph.

4.	Look at lines 40–48. Identify, **in your own words** as far as possible, **six** reasons for *Fortnite's* success compared to PUBG.	6

This is another question which requires you to "locate and translate". Again, it's quite easy to find the correct parts of the paragraph:

1. "Epic Games is one of the industry's oldest outfits, experienced in building and maintaining online competitive video games since the dawn of the internet."
2. "PUBG's updates have been slow and unexciting"
3. "*Fortnite's* updates launch with military-grade regularity"
4. "have introduced a flurry of new items"
5. "and wild, one-off game modes (50 v 50, Sniper rifles only)"
6. "The game's aesthetic . . . has helped convince parents that this is a world of harmless, cartoonish violence"
7. "PUBG, by contrast, is brown and gory"

Now all you have to do is select five of them and turn them into your own words. You would get 1 mark for each one you get right. Let's say you pick 1, 2, 3, 5, 6 and 7. Six bullet points will do nicely. Your answer might look like this:

- the company behind Fortnite has a long and successful tradition in creating and looking after games online
- players have had to wait for changes and additions to PUBG and when they do happen they are uninspired or boring
- improvements to Fortnite happen with a very reliable frequency
- unique and crazy variations of the game
- the design of Fortnite has reassured anxious parents
- the design of PUBG looks dull and violent (and perhaps worryingly realistic)

5.	Look at lines 56–64. Identify, **in your own words, two** reasons why players "aggressively perform a variety of dance moves" (lines 62–63).	2
	Another locate and translate task. You should see that the two reasons are "bonding or antagonism". You would get 1 mark for turning each one into your own words. Your answer might look like this:	
	They do it to make connections with fellow players or to provoke competitors.	
6.	Look at lines 65–74. Summarise, **in your own words** as far as possible, the nature of the *Fortnite* "business model".	4
	You should make **four** key points in your answer.	
	Locate and translate again. You should have spotted the following in the passage:	
	1. "quietly revolutionary"	
	2. "free to download"	
	3. "selling digital costumes, known as skins, to the players"	
	4. "Each day a new wardrobe is put up for sale on the game's storefront, for a few pounds apiece"	
	5. "Players can dress their digital avatar as a ninja, a medieval knight, an Olympic skier, or a skeleton, to name but a few, and in this way stand out from the crowd."	
	6. "it is through their fashion work that the game makes its money"	
	Now choose four of the above and rewrite them using your own words. Let's say you chose 1, 2, 4 and 6. Your answer would look like this:	
	• *the game is ground-breaking but not in an obvious or well publicised way*	
	• *it doesn't cost anything to put it on your device*	
	• *new clothes for characters don't cost much and are made available on a regular basis*	
	• *the profits are made in selling costumes to players*	
7.	Look at lines 92–96. Select any **two** expressions from these lines and explain how they contribute to the passage's effective conclusion.	4
	All you have to do here is quote two expressions (which might be single words or small groups of words) from the final paragraph (1 mark each) and then explain how they help to make the end of the passage effective (1 mark each). You could quote any two of the following:	
	• "dramatic scale of the game's success"	
	• "$100m prize pool for *Fortnite* tournaments"	
	• "other developers rush to create their own *Battle Royales*"	
	• "increasingly likely that *Fortnite* will be the last man standing" and then add suitable explanations. For example:	

"dramatic scale of the game's success" sums up the main idea of the passage – the huge popularity of Fortnite.

or

"$100m prize pool for Fortnite tournaments" repeats the impressive statistic mentioned earlier in the passage.

or

"other developers rush to create their own Battle Royales" suggests the speed that other games companies are operating at to copy the success of this sort of game.

or

"increasingly likely that Fortnite will be the last man standing" describes the game itself as if it were a winning competitor in Fortnite – a reference to the main aim of the game – suggests Fortnite will defeat the competition.

Now you can try a **Reading for understanding, analysis and evaluation** paper yourself.

Schools are destroying the power of stories

In this extract, the author Frank Cottrell Boyce argues that the transformative power of reading is under threat in an education system obsessed with targets and literacy.

Both the government and the arts agencies have recently begun to talk about the economic importance of culture – by which they mean the West End or the film industry. But we need to understand how culture happens. It always floats on a sea of favours and loyalties.
5   Even a massive West End hit like *War Horse* begins with Michael Morpurgo kindly inviting city children to his farm and watching how they related to the horses. If you try and do it for money you end up with *Viva Forever!*. Or *Viva Six Weeks*. And the same is true of the individual reading experience.

10   I visit many schools. I see amazing, creative work being done – especially in primary schools. But I have a nagging fear that in encouraging literacy we are killing the pleasure of reading. I love visiting schools. There's a humbling, Homeric magic in the sight of a crowd of children sitting down waiting to listen to your story. A few
15   months ago, however, a lovely young NQT stepped between me and that crowd and said: 'Now we are very lucky to have Frank with us today. We're going to use our Listening Skills (she touched her ears) to try and spot his Wow Words (what?) and his Connectives so that we can appreciate how he builds the story.' Imagine going on a date
20   with her. 'We're going to have some proteins. Some carbs – not too many – and conversation. If you make me laugh, that's a physical reaction so it puts you on the erotic spectrum and you might get lucky.'

But an encounter with a story should be every bit as unpredictable,
dangerous, full of potential and fear as a first date. My mailbox
25   nowadays is filled with A4 envelopes containing nicely illustrated
letters from year 6 classes. Thirty letters telling me that their favourite
author is me and can I answer some questions. They're nearly all the
same questions. Time and time again I come across teachers reading
a story and then asking immediately for some kind of feedback. A
30   piece of 'creative writing' 'inspired by' the story. Some opinions
about character and wow words. Something to show the parents or
the school inspectors. It pollutes the reading experience by bringing
something transactional into play. It destroys pleasure.

Whenever I talk about this I get the feeling that people are suspicious
35   of the idea of pleasure. They put it in the same category as fun or
distraction. Pleasure is different. Pleasure is a profound and potent
form of attention, a kind of slow thinking. Pleasure anchors an idea or
an image or a concept in your mind and keeps it there for years and
years, allowing you to bring to bear on it not just your intellect but all
40   your other mental qualities – excitement, nostalgia, misunderstanding,
familiarity – until it comes out. When I offer you a story I don't want
you to come back to me with a description of how I did it. I don't think
of my reader as a trainee writer. I'm hoping that it stays in your mind
and comes out again in ways I could never have predicted – as an
45   engineering idea, as a cake, as a hug that you give your dad.

I want to offer some practical suggestions about how to create this
possibility. Read aloud. Just do it. As a treat. We think of reading as a
solitary activity but some of my most important reading experiences
were very much shared. Sister Paul reading to us in year 6 when we
50   had been good. Jackanory on TV. And for my children – rushing home
with the new Harry Potter to read it that very night like a million other
children. I work with an organisation called The Reader, which runs
reading groups for people in schools, in drug rehab, in prison, in
nursing homes. The results are astonishing. The important thing about
55   these groups is that no one is asked to say anything. Just to take the
story and keep it in your brain.

While we were working on the London 2012 Olympic opening
ceremony, Danny Boyle met David Hockney and talked to him about
Humphrey Jennings's *Pandaemonium* – a book I'd given Danny which
60   evokes the industrial revolution and is filled with the clanking of
machines, the yells of protests, tears of goodbye, cries of excitement
and whispers of conspiracy. Hockney gave us this amazing image to
think about. He said, imagine this, the sun pouring down energy from
the beginning of time, energy that went into algae and into the leaves
65   of trees, which then sank into the earth and fossilised. What is coal or
peat but the stored memory of millions upon millions of uninhabited

summers? When the industrial revolution came along, someone opened a hole in the ground and reversed that process. That energy poured out and was harnessed and turned into engines and rockets

70 and aeroplanes and central heating and motor cars, unleashing this wave of incredible creativity.

That's how it should be with stories. They should be sunlight pouring down upon your head and being stored as energy until the day you need them. Whenever we ask for something in return, they are taking

75 that powerful charge and earthing it. Wasting it into the ground. May I take this opportunity to wish you all endless sunlight.

Extract from Frank Cottrell Boyce's David Fickling Lecture,
The Guardian, 17 October 2014

	Total marks — 30 Attempt ALL questions	Marks
1.	Explain fully why the metaphor 'It always floats on a sea of favours and loyalties' (line 4) is effective here.	2
2.	Look at lines 10–14, and explain in your own words what the writer likes about visiting schools.	2
3.	Look at lines 14–22. Explain the writer's attitude to the introduction given by the NQT, and how **two** examples of the language used make this clear.	5
4.	Look at lines 23–32, and identify in your own words three points the writer makes about what an 'encounter' with a story should and shouldn't be.	3
5.	By referring to the sentence in lines 34–35 ('Whenever …'), explain how it helps to provide a link between the writer's ideas at this point in the passage.	2
6.	Look at lines 36–41, and by referring to three examples of the writer's language, explain how the writer makes clear his views about what pleasure is. You should refer to at least **two different** features such as word choice, imagery, sentence structure, etc.	6
7.	Look at lines 46–56, and identify, **in your own words** as far as possible, **four** points the writer makes in these lines about reading.	4
8.	Look at lines 57–71, and explain how **one** feature of the writer's sentence structure and **one** example of the writer's word choice are used to highlight important points.	4
9.	Select any expression in the final paragraph (lines 72–76), and explain how it contributes to the passage's effective conclusion.	2

Check your answers online at www.leckieandleckie.co.uk.

On your own

As a final exercise, read the following and highlight or underline all the examples of the sorts of techniques we've looked at in this chapter. You'll be surprised at how skilled you have become in spotting them. As well as identifying them, think about the sorts of comments you might make about their effect. The article was written after an announcement that the Bayeux Tapestry was coming to the UK on loan from France.

The Bayeux Tapestry: is it any good?

If you want to know why the Bayeux Tapestry truly matters, why it is one of the world's great works of art and not just a corny bit of British heritage, the place to start is not the famous scene of Harold getting it in the eye at the Battle of Hastings, or even the wondrous image of
5   Halley's comet that was embroidered 600 years before Halley, but a far more unsettling detail: a depiction of a war atrocity.

As the Normans establish a beachhead on the south coast, two men are setting fire to a Saxon house. You can tell from their dull disengaged eyes they are only following orders. In front of the blazing
10   building, on a smaller scale than the burly arsonists, a woman holds her boy's hand as she asks for humanity with a dignified, civilised gesture.

The Bayeux Tapestry is not just a fascinating document of a decisive battle in British history. It is one of the richest, strangest, most
15   immediate and unexpectedly subtle depictions of war ever created. That burning house is not the only detail that undercuts the myth of chivalry. At the height of the battle, the lower margin of the 70-metre comic strip – which started out as a parade of bizarre beasts – becomes a carpet of dead bodies, with gorily depicted wounds

20 (one man is headless). Horses are also shown to be war's victims. As they rush into the fray, two take terrible tumbles, landing on their heads and necks. Another horse runs wild with terror among mutilated human corpses.

Not a single horror of war is hidden. Nor are its little ironies. Bishop
25 Odo of Bayeux, half-brother to William the Conqueror, wades into the heart of the fighting with a huge wooden club. As a churchman he can't wield a sword, but there's nothing in the Bible about braining people with oak.

The 'pacifist' details in the Bayeux Tapestry strike some viewers as so
30 subversive that it must have been made in Britain, by Anglo-Saxon women who filled it with seditious subtexts. That's a Brexity long shot. The earliest records of the tapestry suggest it has always been in Normandy. Besides, its honesty about war is part of a bigger picture that paints (sorry, stitches) Duke William as a big-hearted, chivalrous
35 hero whose kindness to the Saxon Harold was repaid by betrayal. What lord should do less when his liegeman breaks an oath than build a fleet, kill his enemy and change the course of British history?

The ambivalence of the Bayeux Tapestry is what makes it so mysterious and majestic. While its creators will always be
40 anonymous, it surely is the perspective of women embroiderers that helps it see so many sides of this story of the male ego run riot. It is both a propagandist narrative of the Norman Conquest and a totally honest exposure of the brutality of battle. Nor is it just black and white – on the contrary, it's red and yellow, brown and blue, and
45 teeming with details of everyday life: workers building ships and castles, a pack of hunting dogs, chain mail, holy relics, roasting meat.

France's loan of this mighty thing to Britain is truly generous and exciting. The Bayeux Tapestry is much more than a chronicle of faraway events or a symbol of national identity. It is a disarmingly
50 human window on a world that is not so different from ours after all – an age of cruelty and comedy, small pleasures and sudden deaths. Like Chaucer's Canterbury Tales, this medieval treasure speaks eloquently to the modern world because it is a true picture of life in all its joy and sorrow. We should be thrilled.

Jonathan Jones, *The Guardian*, 17 January 2018

Section 1 – Scottish texts

This part of the National 5 exam is designed to test your ability to understand, analyse and evaluate an extract taken from one of the Scottish set texts. The SQA intends to refresh this list every few years. For the next few years of this exam, the Scottish set texts are as follows:

Drama

Bold Girls by Rona Munro
Sailmaker by Alan Spence
Tally's Blood by Ann Marie Di Mambro

Prose

Short stories by Iain Crichton Smith
- 'The Red Door'
- 'The Telegram'
- 'Mother and Son'
- 'Home'

Hieroglyphics and Other Stories by Anne Donovan
- 'All that Glisters'
- 'Away in a Manger'
- 'Dear Santa'
- 'Hieroglyphics'

The Testament of Gideon Mack by James Robertson
The Strange Case of Dr Jekyll and Mr Hyde by Robert Louis Stevenson
The Cone-Gatherers by Robin Jenkins

Poetry

Carol Ann Duffy
- 'War Photographer'
- 'Valentine'
- 'Originally'
- 'Mrs Midas'
- 'In Mrs Tischer's Class'
- 'The Way My Mother Speaks'

Edwin Morgan

- 'In the Snack Bar'
- 'Trio'
- 'Good Friday'

- 'Winter'
- 'Glasgow 5 March 1971'
- 'Glasgow Sonnet No. 1'

Norman MacCaig

- 'Assisi'
- 'Visiting Hour'
- 'Aunt Julia'

- 'Basking Shark'
- 'Hotel Room, 12th Floor'
- 'Brooklyn Cop'

Jackie Kay

- 'My Grandmother's Houses'
- 'Lucozade'
- 'Gap Year'

- 'Keeping Orchids'
- 'Old Tongue'
- 'Whilst Leila Sleeps'

You'll notice that the requirement is to study a novel or a play or four short stories or six poems.

Exactly what you study will very much depend on the decisions made by the English teachers at your school. You might, for example, study one of the set texts, one of the groups of poems, and a play and some short stories not on the list. Or you might study two of the set texts during your National 5 course, which would allow you to choose between at least two Scottish set text questions in the exam.

In the exam, you must deal with two different genres. So, for example, you could answer a question on Scottish texts using poetry but then would have to base your critical essay on a prose, drama, film and TV or language topic. In one of the only legitimate 'short cuts' in the exam, you can use the printed Scottish text as the subject of your critical essay *as long as you have not answered on that genre in part 1 of the paper.*

Possible combinations in the critical reading paper	
Question on Scottish text	**Critical essay**
Drama	Prose, Poetry, Film and TV Drama, Language
Prose	Drama, Poetry, Film and TV Drama, Language
Poetry	Drama, Prose, Film and TV Drama, Language

In the questions on Scottish texts part of the critical reading paper, individual questions are worth between 2 and 8 marks and the total number of possible marks is 20. You will be asked questions about the extract printed in the exam paper and about your wider knowledge of the text(s).

You should spend a maximum of 45 minutes on this part of the exam. You should always do this part of the critical reading paper first – if it takes you less than 45 minutes to complete it then that will free up more time for you to plan and write the critical essay.

How to deal with the different types of question in the Scottish texts section

A lot of the questions worth 2, 3 or 4 marks are very similar to the sorts of questions asked in the **Reading for understanding, analysis and evaluation** paper. The 8-mark question that appears at the end of each group of questions requires a slightly different approach – we'll look at that later.

Let's look first of all at some of the questions from the SQA 2017 paper.

Using your own words as far as possible, identify **four** things you learn about the women's lives in this extract. *Bold Girls*	4
Look at lines 12–20. By referring to **two** examples of language, explain how the writer makes clear Duror's feelings towards the cone-gatherers. *The Cone-Gatherers*	2
Look at lines 3–18. Using your own words as far as possible, identify **three** things we learn about the Devil. *The Testament of Gideon Mack*	3
Look at lines 13–18. By referring to **two** examples of language, explain how the poet makes it clear that the war photographer has been strongly affected by his experiences. *Carol Ann Duffy*	4
Look at lines 11–14. By referring to **one** example of language, explain how the poet suggests the idea of innocence. *Edwin Morgan*	2
Look at lines 30–36 ('But I … unanswered'). How effective do you find these lines as a conclusion to the poem? You should refer to **one** example from these lines, and to the language **and/or** ideas of the rest of the poem. *Norman MacCaig*	2

You can see that there are questions that require you to answer using your **own words** and questions that require you to identify an **example of the writer's language** and comment on it. There are also sometimes questions that are more 'evaluative', like the MacCaig example above. No matter which text you have chosen to answer on, all the questions can be answered by using a number of common approaches.

Type of question	What you have to do
Own words	If you are asked to use your own words to identify three or four things from the extract, then simply **locate** them on the page and **translate** them into your own words. You can use bullet points in your answer. You would get one mark for each correct point you made. Find the evidence in the printed text and then highlight or underline it. Then construct the answer using your own words. Your answer to the *Bold Girls* question printed above might look like this: • The women speak openly to each other • The women help each other out • Marie and Cassie are wary of Deirdre • There is tension between Cassie and Deirdre Sometimes you might be asked to 'summarise the main events in this extract', particularly if you are dealing with a drama or prose extract. To answer this you would take the same approach. Ask yourself what the three or four key things that happen in the extract are. What happens at the start? What happens after that? Does something happen as a result of this? What happens at the end? Highlight or underline them and then turn them into your own words in a bullet point list.
Example of language	The first thing you have to do is to **quote** or **refer** to the example of language being used for 1 mark and then provide an **appropriate comment** for 1 mark. You will notice this follows the same pattern as the way marks are allocated in the **Reading for understanding, analysis and evaluation** paper. An 'example of language' might be *any* of the following: • a single word or group of words • an example of particular word choice • an image • sentence structure • punctuation • sound or any other technique used by the writer. An 'appropriate comment' will depend on the question being asked. The word 'suggests' is often a useful one to use. Your answer to the Carol Ann Duffy question printed above might look like this: The short dramatic sentence 'Something is happening' suggests a powerful memory is coming back to him. 'twists before his eyes' suggests the image is an uncomfortable or painful one.

	It doesn't matter which Scottish text you are dealing with; the same principles apply to all of them. An answer to the Edwin Morgan question printed above might look like this:
	'white' suggests something pure or untainted.
	'fresh' suggests something new and unspoiled.
	Remember that you don't need to write great long sentences in your answer! Stick to what it is you are being asked to do.
	Remember also that sometimes the question might refer to a specific technique such as word choice or sentence structure rather than just 'language'. You should answer this in the same way as the more general questions on language: with a **quote plus comment**, e.g.
	'horrid thundering' suggests David was very worried.
	or
	The list in lines 25–28 suggests the large number of dangers faced by the characters.
How effective ... ?	If you are asked **how effective** you find something then make sure you answer that part of the question! Make an evaluative statement. It's always easier to argue that something **is** very effective and then give reasons (after all, these texts have been chosen because they are all effective – they are all high-quality pieces of literature!). Your evidence to support your evaluative statement should again take the form of **quote plus comment**. Your answer to the Norman MacCaig question printed above might look like this:
	These lines are a very effective conclusion to the poem. The repetition in 'getting angry, getting angry' echoes the other examples of this technique earlier in the poem such as 'very loud and very fast'.

Look at this brief summary of the above points:

Type of question	What you have to do
Own words	Locate and translate
Example of language (including questions on specific features)	Quote plus comment
How effective ... ?	Say it's effective (or otherwise) and then quote plus comment for evidence

The 8-mark question

The 8-mark question requires a slightly different approach. Let's look at some examples:

By referring to this extract and to elsewhere in the play, show how the character of Davie is presented.	**8**
By referring to this extract and to at least one other story, show how Donovan creates convincing characters.	**8**
With reference to this poem and at least one other poem by Morgan, show how the use of setting is a significant feature.	**8**

You'll see from the wording that these questions test your knowledge of both the printed poem or extract and your knowledge of the other poems/stories/rest of the novel or play. The question also asks you about a feature that the printed text has in common with the other poems/stories/rest of the novel or play.

There is no clue in the question about how much you have to write about the printed text and how much about the other text(s) but if we look at how this question is marked, then we can find a suitable way to structure an answer.

The SQA marking instructions for this question are as follows:

Candidates may choose to answer in **bullet points** in this final question, or write a number of linked statements. There is **no requirement** to write a 'mini essay'.

Up to 2 marks can be achieved for identifying elements of commonality as identified in the question.

A further 2 marks can be achieved for **reference to the extract given**.

4 additional marks can be awarded for similar references to **at least one part of the text**.

In practice this means: **Identification of commonality (2)** (e.g. theme, central relationship, importance of setting, use of imagery, development in characterisation, use of personal experience, use of narrative style, or any other key element).

From the extract:

1 x relevant reference to technique (1) **1 x** appropriate comment (1)
OR
1 x relevant reference to idea (1) **1 x** appropriate comment (1)
OR
1 x relevant reference to feature (1) **1 x** appropriate comment (1)
OR
1 x relevant reference to text (1) **1 x** appropriate comment (1)

(maximum of 2 marks only for discussion of extract)

From at least one other part of the text:

as above (x 2) for **up to 4 marks**

SQA marking instructions 2017

What does this mean? It means that the best way to structure your answer is as follows:

1. The first section is the 'statement of commonality' – a broad general statement worth 2 marks. Say something about what the printed poem or extract has in common with another of the set poems or stories or the rest of the novel or play. This must relate to the aspect of the text included in the question. The example given below should help you.

2. The second section is your analysis of the printed poem or extract worth 2 marks. Quote plus comment.

3. The third section is your analysis of another of the set poems or stories or the rest of the novel or play worth 4 marks. Two quotes/references plus comments.

An answer to the Anne Donovan question above might look like this:

Statement of Commonality

In 'Zimmerobics' Miss Knight is a convincing character as Anne Donovan shows us her thoughts and feelings about taking part in the exercise class. In the same way, Claire in 'All that Glisters' is a convincing portrait of a young girl facing up to the death of her father.

Extract

'I hadn't felt like this for years' gives the reader a clear sense of Miss Knight's pleasure in taking part and how the class has had a positive effect on her.

<u>Other story</u>

In 'All that Glisters' Claire uses Scots dialect words such as 'Thon wee wifie ...'. This helps to make her character realistic and lets us understand how she thinks.

Claire's closeness to her father is clear when he calls her 'a sight for sore eyes'. The way she tries to cheer him up when he is ill is very believable and typical of what a caring daughter would do.

On the following pages you will find a selection of questions on Scottish texts for practice. It's worth looking at them all – even the ones you are not studying. This will help to reinforce the principles of how to answer each kind of question.

EXAM TIP

Remember that just like in the **Reading for understanding, analysis and evaluation** paper, you only get marks for what you get right – no marks are taken off for anything you get wrong. So it's always worth providing a bit more evidence than the question asks for – but only if you have time to do so. For instance, say the question asked you to refer to two examples of language, there would be no penalty if you referred to three. Then even if one was incorrect and two were correct, you would still get full marks for that answer.

Bold Girls by Rona Munro

Nora and Cassie fall silent.

Marie goes to the kitchen area, opens some crisps, puts them in a bowl, brings them out and sets them down.

Nora and Cassie stare at their drinks.

  5 **CASSIE**   I never hated you.
           Nora scrubs one fierce hand over her eyes but gives no sign she's heard.
                  I just wanted you to make it happen different.
     NORA   Well you'll need to go to some other place where they make the world different, Cassie.
 10 **CASSIE**   Well so I will.
     NORA   You do that.
     CASSIE   I will. I'm leaving.
     NORA   Though it seems to me there's not a place in the world that is different.
 15 **CASSIE**   Well I'll write and tell you.
     NORA   Oh she's got her flight booked, Marie.
     CASSIE   Tell her, Marie.
     MARIE   It's not for me to tell her, Cassie.
     CASSIE   Mummy, I've two hundred pounds saved and I'm getting out.
 20 **NORA**   Oh.

No one says anything else for a second.
              So you've got yourself a flat?
CASSIE   No. I'm leaving Belfast.
NORA   What?
25 **CASSIE** I'm getting on a ferry and I'm getting out.
NORA   What are you saying to me, Cassie?
CASSIE   How many ways do you want me to say it!
There is a pause.
NORA   Well, where are you going?
30 **CASSIE** I'll see where I get to. I'm telling you though I'm not going to
              be one of those that go out on one boat and home on the next
              with their luck all spent. I'm leaving, Mummy.
NORA   And what about your children?
CASSIE   They'll be better off out of here.
35 **NORA**   Are you going to just tear them out by the roots and drag them
              along after you?
CASSIE   No... I...
NORA   To live God knows where on two hundred pound?
CASSIE   I'll send for them... (*Catching Marie's eye*) Oh don't look at
40   me Marie.
NORA   Oh don't come it with your tall tales again, Cassie. Two
              hundred pounds indeed.
CASSIE   Oh is it proof you're wanting? Here then. (*She gets up and goes
              to Michael's picture.*)
45 **MARIE** Cassie what are you doing?
*Cassie feels behind it, stops then starts running her hand frantically over
the back of the picture.*
              What are you doing to Michael?
*Cassie pulls it off the wall and looks at the back of it. She stares at it for a
50 minute then turns to Marie.*
CASSIE   Where is it?
MARIE   What?
CASSIE   My money. Where'd you put it Marie?
MARIE   I never touched a penny of yours, Cassie!
55 **CASSIE** You were the only one knew I had it.
MARIE   I never knew you'd hidden it up the back of Michael!
CASSIE   I had to put it through here; have you seen the way she dusts?
              (*She points at Nora.*)
MARIE   Well I never touched your money, Cassie.
60 **CASSIE** Oh Jesus, someone's lifted it. (*She collapses back into her chair,
              still clutching Michael's picture.*) They've taken my money off
              me! (*She bows her head. She seems about to cry.*)

> *Nora and Marie look at each other*
> **NORA** (*Crossing to her*) Cassie?
> 65 *Cassie shakes her head.*
> (*Hesitating a moment*)
> Och you're not crying, are you?
> *Cassie just looks at her.*
> Well, what age are you to be making up daydreams and
> 70 spoiling your face crying for them. Come on, now.

Questions

1.	Look at lines 1–4. By referring to two examples, show how the stage directions suggest key ideas about the characters.	4
2.	Look at lines 5–20. By referring to two examples of language, show how the writer suggests the conflict between Nora and Cassie.	4
3.	Look at lines 33–42. By referring to two examples of language, show how the writer presents Nora and Cassie's differing views about what will happen to Cassie's children.	4
4.	With close reference to this extract and to elsewhere in the play, explain how the writer explores the theme of hopes and dreams.	8

'The Telegram' by Iain Crichton Smith

The two women — one fat and one thin — sat at the window of the thin woman's house drinking tea and looking down the road which ran through the village. They were like two birds, one a fat domestic bird perhaps, the other more aquiline, more gaunt, or, to be precise, more like
5 a buzzard.

It was wartime and though the village appeared quiet, much had gone on in it. Reverberations from a war fought far away had reached it: many of its young men had been killed, or rather drowned, since nearly all of them had joined the Navy, and their ships had sunk in seas which they
10 had never seen except on maps which hung on the walls of the local school which they all had at one time or another unwillingly attended. One had been drowned on a destroyer after a leave during which he had told his family that he would never come back again. (Or at least that was the rumour in the village which was still, as it had always been, a
15 superstitious place.) Another had been drowned during the pursuit of the *Bismarck*.

What the war had to do with them the people of the village did not know. It came on them as a strange plague, taking their sons away and then killing them, meaninglessly, randomly. They watched the road often for
20 the telegrams.

The telegrams were brought to the houses by the local elder who, clad in black, would walk along the road and then stop at the house to which the telegram was directed. People began to think of the telegram as a strange missile pointed at them from abroad. They did not know what to
25 associate it with, certainly not with God, but it was a weapon of some kind, it picked a door and entered it, and left desolation just like any other weapon.

The two women who watched the street were different, not only physically but socially. For the thin woman's son was a sub-lieutenant in the Navy
30 while the fat woman's son was only an ordinary seaman. The fat woman's son had to salute the thin woman's son. One got more pay than the other, and wore better uniform. One had been at university and had therefore become an officer, the other had left school at the age of fourteen.

When they looked out the window they could see cows wandering lazily
35 about, but little other movement. The fat woman's cow used to eat the thin woman's washing and she was looking out for it but she couldn't see it. The thin woman was not popular in the village. She was an incomer from another village and had only been in this one for thirty years or so. The fat woman had lived in the village all her days; she was a native. Also
40 the thin woman was ambitious: she had sent her son to university though she only had a widow's pension of ten shillings a week.

As they watched they could see at the far end of the street the tall man in black clothes carrying in his hand a piece of yellow paper. This was a bare village with little colour and therefore the yellow was both strange
45 and unnatural.

The fat woman said: 'It's Macleod again.'

'I wonder where he's going today.'

They were both frightened for he could be coming to their house. And so they watched him and as they watched him they spoke feverishly as if by
50 speaking continually and watching his every move they would be able to keep from themselves whatever plague he was bringing.

Questions

1.	Look at lines 1–5.	
	By referring to two examples, explain how the writer's use of imagery conveys a sense of the appearance and the personality of the two women.	4
2.	Look at lines 17–20.	
	By referring to one example, explain how the writer's use of language suggests the villagers' feelings about the war.	2

3.	Look at lines 14–15, '… the village which was still, as it had always been, a superstitious place'. How does the women's behaviour described in a *later* part of the extract illustrate the superstitious nature of the villagers?	2
4.	Look at lines 28–33. Using your own words as far as possible, explain the differences between the two sons.	2
5.	Look at lines 42–45. By referring to one example of the writer's language, show how references to colour are significant at this point in the extract.	2
6.	By referring to this story, and to at least one other story by Iain Crichton Smith, show how he makes effective use of setting in his writing.	8

'All that Glisters'
by Anne Donovan

Thon wee wifie brung them in, the wan that took us for two days when Mrs McDonald wis aff. She got us tae make Christmas cards wi coloured cardboard and felties, which is a bit much when we're in second year, but naebdy wis gonnae say anythin cos it's better than daein real work.

5 Anyway ah like daein things like that and made a right neat wee card for ma daddy wi a Christmas tree and a robin and a bit a holly on it.

That's lovely, dear. What's your name?

Clare.

Would you like to use the glitter pens?

10 And she pulled oot the pack fae her bag.

Ah'd never seen them afore, When ah wis in Primary Four the teacher gied us tubes of glitter but it wis quite messy. Hauf the stuff ended up on the flair and it wis hard tae make sure you got the glue in the right places. But these pens were different cos the glue wis mixed in wi the glitter so

15 you could jist draw with them. It wis pure brilliant, so it wis. There wis four colours, rid, green, gold and silver, and it took a wee while tae get the hang of it. You had tae be careful when you squeezed the tube so's you didnae get a big blob appearin at wanst, but efter a few goes ah wis up an runnin.

20 And when ah'd finished somethin amazin hud happened. Ah cannae explain whit it wis but the glitter jist brought everythin tae life, gleamin and glisterin agin the flat cardboard. It wis like the difference between a Christmas tree skinklin wi fairy lights an wan lyin deid an daurk in a corner.

Ma daddy wis dead chuffed. He pit the card on the bedside table
25 and smiled.

Fair brightens up this room, hen.

It's good tae find sumpn that cheers him up even a wee bit because ma
daddy's really sick. He's had a cough fur as long as ah can remember,
and he husny worked fur years, but these past three month he cannae
30 even get oot his bed. Ah hear him coughin in the night sometimes and
it's different fae the way he used tae cough, comes fae deeper inside him
somehow, seems tae rack his hale body fae inside oot. When ah come in
fae school ah go and sit wi him and tell him aboot whit's happened that
day, but hauf the time he looks away fae me and stares at a patch on the
35 downie cover where there's a coffee stain that ma ma cannae wash oot.
He used tae work strippin oot buildins and he wis breathin in stour aw
day, sometimes it wis that bad he'd come hame wi his hair and his claes
clartit wi it. He used tae kid on he wis a ghost and walk in the hoose wi
his airms stretched oot afore him and ah'd rin and hide unner the stair,
40 watchin him walk by wi the faint powdery whiteness floatin roon his heid.

He never knew there wis asbestos in the dust, never knew a thing aboot it
then, nane of them did. Noo he's an expert on it, read up aw these books
tae try and unnerstaun it fur the compensation case. Before he got really
sick he used tae talk aboot it sometimes.

45 *You see, hen, the word asbestos comes fae a Greek word that means
indestructible. That's how they use it fur fireproofin — the fire cannae
destroy it.*

*You mean if you wore an asbestos suit you could walk through fire and it
widnae hurt you?*

50 *Aye. In the aulden days they used tae bury the royals in it. They cried it
the funeral dress of kings.*

Questions

1.	Look at lines 1–6.	
	Using your own words as far as possible, explain the narrator's reaction to being asked 'tae make Christmas cards wi coloured cardboard and felties'.	2
2.	Look at lines 7–10.	
	Suggest two reasons for the difference between the language the writer gives the supply teacher and the language given to Clare.	2

3.	Look at lines 11–23.	
	By referring to two examples of language, explain how the writer suggests Clare's reaction to the glitter pens.	4
4.	Look at lines 27–40.	
	Using your own words as far as possible, identify four things we learn about Clare's father.	4
5.	By referring to this story, and to at least one other story by Anne Donovan, show how the writer presents relationships between characters.	8

The Strange Case of Dr Jekyll and Mr Hyde by Robert Louis Stevenson

In this extract from Chapter 4, 'The Carew Murder Case', a maidservant has witnessed a murder.

It was two o'clock when she came to herself and called for the police. The murderer was gone long ago; but there lay his victim in the middle of the lane, incredibly mangled. The stick with which the deed had been done, although it was of some rare and very tough and heavy wood, had
5 broken in the middle under the stress of this insensate cruelty; and one splintered half had rolled in the neighbouring gutter–the other, without doubt, had been carried away by the murderer. A purse and a gold watch were found upon the victim; but no cards or papers, except a sealed and stamped envelope, which he had been probably carrying to the post, and
10 which bore the name and address of Mr. Utterson.

This was brought to the lawyer the next morning, before he was out of bed; and he had no sooner seen it, and been told the circumstances, than he shot out a solemn lip. 'I shall say nothing till I have seen the body,' said he; 'this may be very serious. Have the kindness to wait while
15 I dress.' And with the same grave countenance he hurried through his breakfast and drove to the police station, whither the body had been carried. As soon as he came into the cell, he nodded.

'Yes,' said he, 'I recognise him. I am sorry to say that this is Sir Danvers Carew.'

20 'Good God, sir,' exclaimed the officer, 'is it possible?' And the next moment his eye lighted up with professional ambition. 'This will make a deal of noise,' he said. 'And perhaps you can help us to the man.' And he briefly narrated what the maid had seen, and showed the broken stick.

25 Mr. Utterson had already quailed at the name of Hyde; but when the stick was laid before him, he could doubt no longer: broken and battered as it was, he recognized it for one that he had himself presented many years before to Henry Jekyll.

'Is this Mr. Hyde a person of small stature?' he inquired.

30 'Particularly small and particularly wicked-looking, is what the maid calls him,' said the officer.

Mr. Utterson reflected; and then, raising his head, 'If you will come with me in my cab,' he said, 'I think I can take you to his house.'

It was by this time about nine in the morning, and the first fog of the
35 season. A great chocolate-coloured pall lowered over heaven, but the
wind was continually charging and routing these embattled vapours;
so that as the cab crawled from street to street, Mr. Utterson beheld a
marvellous number of degrees and hues of twilight; for here it would
be dark like the back-end of evening; and there would be a glow of
40 a rich, lurid brown, like the light of some strange conflagration; and
here, for a moment, the fog would be quite broken up, and a haggard
shaft of daylight would glance in between the swirling wreaths. The
dismal quarter of Soho seen under these changing glimpses, with its
muddy ways, and slatternly passengers, and its lamps, which had never
45 been extinguished or had been kindled afresh to combat this mournful
reinvasion of darkness, seemed, in the lawyer's eyes, like a district of
some city in a nightmare. The thoughts of his mind, besides, were of
the gloomiest dye; and when he glanced at the companion of his drive,
he was conscious of some touch of that terror of the law and the law's
50 officers, which may at times assail the most honest.

Questions

1.	Using your own words as far as possible, summarise the main events in this extract.	
	You should make **four** key points in your answer.	4
2.	Look at lines 1–10.	
	Explain how **one** example of the writer's language suggests the nature of the attack on the victim.	2
3.	Look at lines 11–24.	
	(a) Explain how **one** example of the writer's language shows Mr. Utterson's feelings at this point in the extract.	2
	(b) Explain how **one** example of the writer's language shows the officer's feelings at this point in the extract.	2
4.	Look at lines 34–50.	
	By referring to **two** examples of the writer's language, show how Stevenson creates a vivid picture of Mr. Utterson's journey through London.	4
5.	By referring to this extract and to elsewhere in the novel, show how Stevenson creates convincing characters.	8

The Cone-Gatherers by Robin Jenkins

In this extract from Chapter 16, Lady Runcie-Campbell runs to where the cone-gatherers are working.

As she ran, and stumbled, climbed fences, jumped over streams, scrambled up banks, and plunged deep into leaves, Lady Runcie-Campbell tried to make her anger against the cone-gatherers grow. Their insolence, independence and their even more outrageous attempt at

5 revenge, resulting in the prolonged danger to her son, were surely just reasons for hating and despising them; for wishing Duror well in his intention to chastise them into decency and obedience; and for vowing, when all this was over, to obliterate the forester's false yellow smile of comprehension and forgiveness by complaining to his superiors so

10 strongly that they must either dismiss him or degrade him. As a mother, as a landowner, as a Christian even, surely she was justified? Yet not for a second of that dreadful journey to the Point did she convince herself. Whatever she ought to feel, anger seemed wrong and unavailing. She kept remembering Roderick's strange chatter that morning about Bhudda;

15 Harry after she'd struck him, and also before he had, trembling with shyness and trepidation, offered to climb the tree; Duror with the naked doll in his fist and the obscene accusations so lusciously on his lips; old Graham at the fir tree stinking so rankly of sweat and whispering so compassionately into her ear; and always, dominating every other

20 memory, the two cone-gatherers leaving the beach hut. Fear, anxiety, love, sorrow, regret, and hope, were in her mind, but not anger.

From the silver fir to the Point took ten minutes; during them she seemed to travel to the furthest limits of her being, there to be baulked by not finding what she had hoped to find, and without which she could never return.

25 Behind her, always at that proper distance, ran Baird, a big red-eared solemn man, who kept thinking what a good thing it was he had, after all, taken Manson with him to the tree. The lady had promised to reward Bob; but it was a recognised rule of the world that if a subordinate was rewarded, his master must be rewarded also, to maintain stations, and of

30 course more handsomely according to his higher degree. In the war, for instance, there were different medals for privates and officers, although they fought in the same battles.

From a bank of whins and bracken she looked down on the promontory. Never had the loch been so potently beautiful: it was as vast, bright,

35 and detailed as in a dream; and there seemed to be a wonderful interpretation, if it could only be known. A warship steamed down the

loch. So intimate a part of the dream was it, she seemed, during those few moments of suspense upon the bank, to know all its crew and what was to be each man's fate in the sea towards which it was bound. There,
40 too, dream-like, were the pines, her favourite trees, making against sea and sky what had always struck her as Scottish gestures, recalling the eerie tormented tragic grandeur of the old native ballads. Gulls, as prodigal of time and sky as she must be parsimonious, flew and shrieked high over them.

45 She could not see any men; they must be hidden by the trees. But as she began to go down the bank, tearing her clothes on the whins and splintering the bracken, she heard the report of a gun, followed by a scream, and then by the quickened wails of the gulls.

As she raced among the pines, making for that gunshot, she prayed that
50 Duror in his madness had not hurt the cone-gatherers, not for their sakes, nor for his, nor for his wife's, but for her son's.

She saw Duror before she saw them. He was walking away among the pine trees with so infinite a desolation in his every step that it was this memory of him, rather than that of the little hunchback dangling from
55 the tree, or that of his brother climbing so frenziedly up into it, which was to torment her sleep for months.

Questions

1.	Look at lines 1–21. By referring to two examples of language, explain how the writer makes clear Lady Runcie-Campbell's state of mind at this point in the novel.	4
2.	Look at lines 25–32. Using your own words as far as possible, explain why Baird is pleased 'he had taken Manson to the tree with him'.	2
3.	Look at lines 33–44. By referring to two examples of language, explain how the writer gives significance to what Lady Runcie-Campbell sees.	4
4.	Look at lines 52–53. Explain how the image '… with so infinite a desolation in his every step' effectively describes Duror's feelings at this point of the story.	2
5.	By referring to this extract, and to elsewhere in the novel, show how Jenkins portrays Lady Runcie-Campbell as a conflicted character.	8

'Originally' by Carol Ann Duffy

> We came from our own country in a red room
> which fell through the fields, our mother singing
> our father's name to the turn of the wheels.
> My brothers cried, one of them bawling *Home,*
> 5   *Home*, as the miles rushed back to the city,
> the street, the house, the vacant rooms
> where we didn't live any more. I stared
> at the eyes of a blind toy, holding its paw.
>
> All childhood is an emigration. Some are slow,
> 10   leaving you standing, resigned, up an avenue
> where no one you know stays. Others are sudden.
> Your accent wrong. Corners, which seem familiar,
> leading to unimagined, pebble-dashed estates, big boys
> eating worms and shouting words you don't understand.
> 15   My parents' anxiety stirred like a loose tooth
> in my head. *I want our own country*, I said.
>
> But then you forget, or don't recall, or change,
> and, seeing your brother swallow a slug, feel only
> a skelf of shame. I remember my tongue
> 20   shedding its skin like a snake, my voice
> in the classroom sounding just like the rest. Do I only think
> I lost a river, culture, speech, sense of first space
> and the right place? Now, *Where do you come from?*
> strangers ask. *Originally?* And I hesitate.

Questions

1.	Look at lines 1–8. By referring to two examples of language, show how the poet presents contrasting moods in these lines.	4
2.	Look at line 9. Using your own words as far as possible, explain what the poet means by 'All childhood is an emigration.'	2

3.	Look at lines 9–12. By referring to two examples of language, show how a contrast between the two types of experience is suggested.	4
4.	Look at lines 15–19. By referring to one example of imagery, explain how it conveys a key idea in the speaker's thoughts or feelings.	2
5.	By referring to this poem, and to at least one other poem by Carol Ann Duffy, show how she makes effective use of striking imagery to convey the central concerns of the texts.	8

'Glasgow 5 March 1971' by Edwin Morgan

> With a ragged diamond
> of shattered plate glass
> a young man and his girl
> are falling backwards into a shop window.
> 5   The young man's face
> is bristling with fragments of glass
> and the girl's leg has caught
> on the broken window
> and spurts arterial blood
> 10   over her wet-look white coat.
> Their arms are starfished out
> braced for impact,
> their faces show surprise, shock
> and the beginning of pain.
> 15   The two youths who have pushed them
> are about to complete the operation
> reaching into the window
> to loot what they can smartly.
> Their faces show no expression.
> 20   It is a sharp, clear night
> in Sauchiehall Street.
> In the background two drivers
> keep their eyes on the road.

Questions

1.	Look at lines 1–4.	
	By referring to one example of language, show these four lines provide an effective opening to the poem.	2
2.	Look at lines 5–10.	
	By referring to one example of language, show how the poet provides a vivid description of either the young man **or** the girl.	2

3.	Look at lines 15–19. By referring to two examples of language, show how the poet suggests the attitude of the two youths to what they are doing.	4
4.	Look at lines 20–23. By referring to two examples of language, show how the poet has created an effective ending to the poem.	4
5.	With reference to this poem and at least one other poem by Morgan, show how the use of setting is a significant feature.	8

'Hotel Room, 12th Floor' by Norman MacCaig

This morning I watched from here
a helicopter skirting like a damaged insect
the Empire State Building, that
jumbo size dentist's drill, and landing
5   on the roof of the PanAm skyscraper.
But now midnight has come in
from foreign places. Its uncivilised darkness
is shot at by a million lit windows, all
ups and acrosses.

10   But midnight is not
so easily defeated. I lie in bed, between
a radio and a television set, and hear
the wildest of warwhoops continually ululating through
the glittering canyons and gulches –
15   police cars and ambulances racing
to the broken bones, the harsh screaming
from coldwater flats, the blood
glazed on sidewalks.

The frontier is never
20   somewhere else. And no stockades
can keep the midnight out.

Questions

1.	Look at lines 1–9. By referring to two examples of language, show how the poet presents the reader with a vivid picture of the city.	4
2.	Look at lines 10–13. By referring to two examples of language, show how the poet presents the reader with contrasting ideas.	4
3.	Look at lines 14–18. By referring to one example of word choice, show how MacCaig suggests the atmosphere or mood of the city at night.	2
4.	Using your own words as far as possible, explain two key ideas in the final stanza.	2
5.	By referring to this poem, and to at least one other poem by MacCaig, show how he makes use of his own experiences as a way of considering wider themes.	8

Section 2 – the critical essay

Once you've got the question on Scottish texts element of the SQA exam out of the way, it's time for Part 2. Part 2 of this paper requires you to write a critical essay.

Key points

- The critical essay tests your skills in understanding, evaluation and analysis.
- You will write **one** critical essay on a text you have studied as part of your course.
- Your essay can be on a drama, prose, poetry, film and TV drama text or on a language topic.
- There will be two questions on each of these genres to choose from.
- You will be expected to complete the essay in around 45 minutes.
- Your essay will be marked out of 20.

Your choice of critical essay question will also depend on which Scottish text you are going to answer on. You cannot use the same genre for both Part 1 and Part 2 of the critical reading question paper.

Let's look at how your essay will be marked. Your marker will allocate your essay to one of five categories and then decide on a final mark within that category. The table on the next page shows the features of a *very good* essay (Category 1) and the features of an essay that is *just good enough* to pass (Category 3).

	Category 1 Essays in this category will be awarded 20, 19 or 18 marks.	Category 3 Essays in this category will be awarded 13, 12, 11 or 10 marks.
The candidate demonstrates:	• a **high degree of familiarity** with the text as a whole • **very good understanding** of the central concerns of the text • a line of thought that is **consistently relevant** to the task	• **some familiarity** with the text as a whole • **some understanding** of the central concerns of the text • a line of thought that is **mostly relevant** to the task
Analysis of the text demonstrates:	• **very sound awareness** of the writer's techniques through analysis, making confident use of critical terminology • **very detailed/thoughtful** explanation of stylistic devices supported by a **range of well-chosen** references and/or quotations	• an **awareness** of the writer's techniques through analysis, making some use of critical terminology • explanation of stylistic devices supported by **some appropriate** reference and/or quotation
Evaluation of the text is shown through:	• a **well-developed** commentary of what has been enjoyed/gained from the text(s), supported by a **range of** well-chosen references to its **relevant** features	• **some** commentary of what has been enjoyed/gained from the text(s), supported by **some appropriate** references to its **relevant** features
The candidate:	• uses language to communicate a line of thought **very clearly** • uses grammar, sentence construction and punctuation that are **consistently** accurate • structures the essay **effectively to enhance** meaning/purpose • uses paragraphing that is **accurate and effective**	• uses language to communicate a line of thought **at first reading** • uses spelling, grammar, sentence construction and punctuation that are **sufficiently** accurate • attempts to structure the essay **in an appropriate way** • uses paragraphing that is **sufficiently accurate**
In summary, the candidate's essay is:	• thorough and precise (very good)	• fairly detailed and relevant (satisfactory)

Make sure that you understand exactly what some of the terms used in the table mean:

Central concerns of the text – These are the main ideas the writer is trying to communicate to the reader.

Line of thought – This means that the points you make in your essay are structured in a clear, relevant and logical fashion.

Critical terminology – You must be able to make confident use of the technical terms appropriate to the genre of the text you are writing about in your essay.

– For **drama** these include: characterisation, setting, language, key incident(s), climax/turning point, plot, structure, narrative technique, theme, ideas, description etc.

– For **prose** these include: characterisation, setting, language, key incident(s), climax/turning point, plot, structure, narrative technique, theme, ideas, description etc.

– For **poetry** these include: word choice, tone, imagery, structure, content, rhythm, theme, sound, ideas etc.

– For **film and TV drama** these include: use of camera, key sequence, characterisation, mise-en-scène, editing, setting, music/sound, effects, plot, dialogue etc.

– For **language** these include: register, accent, dialect, slang, jargon, vocabulary, tone, abbreviation etc.

Once you have decided which critical essay question you are going to answer, you must be certain exactly what it is you are being asked to do.

Look at this example:

> Choose a play that contains a strong female character.
>
> Briefly describe the character's role in the play and go on to explain how her strength is revealed to the audience.

Your first ask is to highlight or <u>underline</u> the key words in the question. Remember to treat the exam paper as your property in the exam and mark it up in any way you find helpful.

> Choose a play that contains a strong female character.
>
> Briefly describe the character's role in the play and go on to explain how her strength is revealed to the audience.

Notice that you are being asked to do **two** things in this essay. Your answer **must** deal with both. In this case you are asked to (briefly) describe what the character does in the play and – the more substantial part of the answer – explain the various ways the playwright shows the character's strength to the reader.

Your second task is to write the plan for the essay. You can use bullet points

- idea no. 1
- idea no. 2
- idea no. 3

or a mind-map (spider diagram).

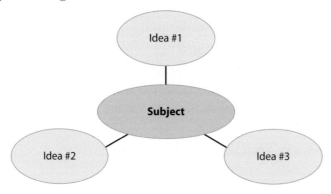

You can use whatever system works best for you. A plan for our strong female character essay might look like this:

Play: *Bold Girls*

Strong female character: Nora

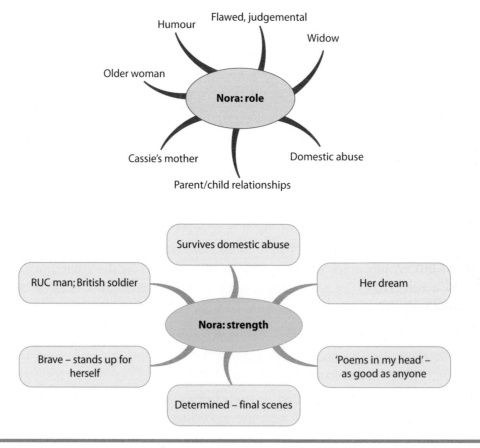

You have to complete the essay in around 45 minutes so you should spend about 5 minutes on planning and most of the remaining 40 on writing. You should also allow a few minutes for giving your essay a final read-over just before time is up.

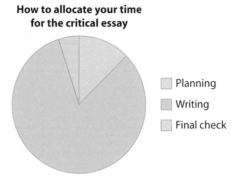

How to allocate your time for the critical essay

- Planning
- Writing
- Final check

The opening paragraph of your essay should refer to the title of the text you are writing about, the author's name and the key words of the task itself (or **TAT: T**itle, **A**uthor, **T**ask).

Each paragraph which then follows should develop the line of thought in your essay. The ideas you have written down in your plan will provide the content for each of these paragraphs.

Remember each paragraph should have a **topic sentence** – a sentence that introduces, highlights or sums up what the paragraph is about. You should provide evidence (a **quotation from** or a **reference to** something in the text) to support the points you make and also explain how this evidence contributes to your argument or line of thought. If it helps, you can think of **PEE** (or **P**oint, **E**vidence, **E**xplanation) as you write.

MacCaig's encounter with the shark makes him think about the past. It 'shoggled me centuries back'. This shows the dramatic effect the incident has on him and forces him to start to reconsider the place of humans in evolution – an important theme in this poem.

You can even use this structure multiple times within each section or paragraph. But be careful not to overdo it; the best essays don't read as if they've been written using a formula.

While you are being taught each text as part of your course you must revise and learn the main ideas (central concerns) of each text, the techniques used by the writer and a selection of appropriate quotations. You must be able to recall these from memory in the exam hall. Do whatever it takes to keep these in your head.

Shorter quotations should be embedded within the rest of the sentence they belong with:

MacCaig's description of the dwarf 'with his hands on backwards' shocks the reader.

Longer quotations should be placed in a separate paragraph on their own.

It is important that you **link** the sections and paragraphs together effectively. Use expressions such as:

- For example
- Because of this …
- As a result … therefore
- In spite of this …
- In the same way …
- Firstly … secondly … thirdly …
- Yet … but …
- Furthermore …
- On the other hand …
- In conclusion … or To sum up …

EXAM TIP

In order to remember quotations:
- underline or highlight appropriate lines in your copy of the text
- choose relevant quotes that can be used in a variety of essays, e.g. ones that might illustrate theme and characterisation
- write quotations on sticky notes and put these where you'll keep seeing them
- put them in your phone (but don't take this into the exam hall)
- test yourself regularly

Your final paragraph should provide an effective conclusion to your essay. In it you should sum up the points you have made and refer again to the key words of the question. This acts as a reminder to your marker that you have written a relevant response. It is vital that you keep to the question you have been set and don't just write down everything you know about a particular text.

Exemplar critical essay

Let's look at how to put all the advice given above into practice. Having thought about and planned your response, here's what the completed essay would look like.

> Choose a play that contains a strong female character.
>
> Briefly describe the character's role in the play and go on to explain how her strength is revealed to the audience.

Your opening paragraph should mention the title and author of your chosen text and refer to the question.

'Bold Girls' by Rona Munro is a play that contains a strong female character. Nora, one of the 'Bold Girls' in the play, is a woman who has managed to survive and keep going despite the experience of her personal life being affected by domestic abuse and her family life being disrupted by The Troubles in Northern Ireland in the 1970s and 80s.

Nora is older than the other three women in the play. She is Cassie's mother and a widow with a son who is in prison, presumably for terrorist offences. Rona Munro uses the character to add humour to the play, to explore the theme of parent and child relationships and to illustrate the theme of domestic violence.

a brief description of the character and her role in the play

In many ways, Nora is a flawed character. She can be quick to judge and is sometimes very cynical. When Deirdre first arrives at Marie's house, Nora thinks she is a glue-sniffer. She also describes the girl, who is probably the mother of her son Martin's child, as 'nothing but a wee hoor'. She has a difficult relationship with her daughter, Cassie, and always seems to compare her unfavourably with her brother Martin: 'Our Martin never grudged me a cigarette'. Cassie acknowledges this when she tells Marie 'I fell out with my mummy on the delivery room floor'.

effective use of quotation to back up the point made

Despite these flaws Rona Munro shows the audience that Nora is also a strong character. This is shown in two of the anecdotes she tells in the play. In one she describes how she stood up to the RUC man who came to arrest Cassie's husband, Joe:

effective link sentence to move the essay forward

'And he says "And who are you?" And I says, "I'm that boy's mother-in-law, before you take him you'll have to answer to me!"'

The audience laughs along with Nora and the other bold girls when she tells of how he then 'knocked her straight through the hedge'. Later in scene two, at

reference to Rona Munro's use of humour

the Club, she describes how one of the Brits who had destroyed her bamboo suite 'with boots like anvils' assaulted her with the result that she had her ribs 'taped up for months'. She has also suffered at the hands of her husband:

'She'd come down in the morning, Marie, and find me crying on the floor with the bruises going black on my face and all she'd say was, "Have you been upsetting daddy again?" Go and fix herself a cup of tea.'

longer quotation placed in a separate paragraph

These lines also show how Rona Munro suggests the relationship between fathers and daughters is different to that between mothers and daughters.

more evidence to support the idea of Nora as a strong character

We are also shown Nora as a strong character when she refuses to give up on her dream of decorating her 'front room' just the way she wants it. The playwright uses Nora's obsession with decorating her house as a symbol of one woman's attempt to impose some sort of order on the chaos of living in Belfast during The Troubles. Just as she destroys Cassie's dream of escape by stealing her £200, Deirdre symbolically destroys Nora's dream by slashing the 'fifteen yards of peach polyester' and 'trampling it till she's breathless'.

evidence of wider knowledge of the text

Even this setback does not get Nora down for long. As the plot moves towards the climactic final scenes of the drama, Nora says defiantly, 'Well I'm going up the town tomorrow. I'm just going to go up the town and buy a piece of what I want. I'll get credit and have my loose covers.'

The audience is left with an image of a woman who has been through a lot and yet still refuses to give in. The skilful characterisation of Nora presents us with a very human character with all the usual human failings and yet someone who has an inner strength and resolve. As Nora tells us herself

reference to an appropriate dramatic technique

a reference back to the question itself – always refer back to the question at the end of your essay

'I've poems in my head as good as anyone.'

> Here is another example of a critical essay. Read through it yourself and see if you can spot the approaches and techniques that have been mentioned so far.

Example

Choose a play that explores an important relationship, e.g. between husband and wife, leader and follower, parent and child.

Describe this relationship and then, by referring to appropriate techniques, explain how the relationship develops.

Macbeth by William Shakespeare explores the important relationship between Macbeth and his wife, Lady Macbeth.

It is clear from early on in the play that the relationship between husband and wife is very close. In the exposition, Macbeth is portrayed by Shakespeare as a fierce warrior who is loyal to King Duncan. We hear Macbeth described as 'brave' in the battle against the rebels and the Norwegians, and Duncan rewards 'noble Macbeth' by making him Thane of Cawdor. Macbeth seems keen to share his successes with his wife. In the letter he writes to Lady Macbeth, he refers to her as 'my dearest partner of greatness' and tells her about the witches' prophecy that he will become King of Scotland. In the same scene, however, Shakespeare gives the audience an insight into what Lady Macbeth thinks about her husband: according to her he is 'too full o' th' milk of human kindness' to go through with the killing of Duncan.

Shakespeare presents us with a clear contrast between the husband and wife in these early scenes. Macbeth seems content just to let things happen: 'If chance will have me King, why, chance may crown me', whereas Lady Macbeth is eager to act on the opportunity being presented:

> 'The raven himself is hoarse
>
> That croaks the fatal entrance of Duncan
>
> Under my battlements.'

It now seems that Lady Macbeth takes charge of the situation. Shakespeare's use of imagery in her speeches with Macbeth – 'look like th'innocent flower, But be the serpent under it' – clearly shows her telling him what to do and also that they must seem to be innocent while doing these evil deeds.

When Macbeth seems to be less keen to go through with the murder of Duncan, Lady Macbeth criticises him and his masculinity: 'When you durst do it, then you were a man' and again it is clear how she is able to manipulate him.

In the key scene immediately following the murder, it is once more Lady Macbeth who takes control of the situation, and Shakespeare presents her as the more dominant partner in the relationship:

> 'Go get some water,
>
> And wash this filthy witness from your hand.
>
> Why did you bring these daggers from the place?
>
> They must lie there: go carry them, and smear
>
> The sleepy grooms with blood.'

Lady Macbeth's confident statement that 'A little water clears us of this deed' is a good example of Shakespeare's use of dramatic irony given the later events in the play. The two of them are now bound together in their guilt although Shakespeare continues to suggest the tensions in their relationship:

> 'My hands are of your colour; but I shame
>
> To wear a heart so white.'

It is perhaps because he feels he has to prove himself that Macbeth does not tell his wife about his plans for Banquo and Fleance.

Lady Macbeth continues to be the strong one in the relationship when she covers up for her husband in the banquet scene after Macbeth sees Banquo's ghost. It is therefore ironic that she is the first one to crack under the pressure of their guilt. She descends into madness and Shakespeare's use of the sleepwalking scene is all the more shocking as it shows how much her character has changed.

Even in her changed state, Macbeth still seems to care for her. He tells the doctor to 'Cure her of that' and to 'cleanse ... that perilous stuff/That weighs upon the heart'. The news of her death prompts him to reflect darkly on life and mortality 'Tomorrow and tomorrow and tomorrow ...'. In this soliloquy the mood is downbeat as Macbeth concludes that 'Life's a walking shadow, a poor player' and is 'a Tale told by an idiot'.

In conclusion we can see that in this tragedy Shakespeare explores the important relationship between Macbeth and Lady Macbeth and uses it to present themes such as love, good and evil, ambition and greed. There is no doubt that Lady Macbeth is one of the factors that lead to Macbeth's downfall. Shakespeare skilfully shows us the closeness between Macbeth and his wife but also the tensions as their relationship develops during the course of the play. At the end of the play the audience perhaps feels little sympathy for 'this dead butcher and his fiend-like Queen'.

You can use the following questions to practise your critical essay writing skills.

Remember that the types of questions you get asked tend to fall into groups. Prepare yourself to write about theme, character, setting, structure, etc.

EXAM TIP

Always practise essays 'against the clock'. Take 45 minutes for each essay.

Practice essay questions

Drama

- Choose a play in which one character mistrusts another character.
  Explain the nature of this mistrust and how it affects the outcome of the play.
- Choose a play that contains a strong female character.
  Briefly describe the character's role in the play and go on to explain how her strength is revealed to the audience.
- Choose a play that explores the theme of survival.
  With reference to appropriate dramatic techniques, show how this theme is presented to the audience.
- Choose a play that relies on more than just dialogue to achieve dramatic effects.
  Explain how the playwright makes use of these techniques to achieve these effects.
- Choose a play that explores the relationship between parents and their children.
  By making reference to specific dramatic techniques, show how the dramatist presents this theme to the audience.
- Choose a play in which the main character is isolated from those around him or her.
  Briefly describe the nature of the isolation and go on to show how this affects the drama as a whole.
- Choose a play in which there is a mixture of sadness and comedy.
  Briefly describe how these elements are presented in the play and go on to show how they add to the overall effectiveness of the drama.
- Choose a play in which a key scene reveals something significant about the main character.
  Briefly describe what happens and go on to show the significance of the scene to the play as a whole.
- Choose a play that you think ends in a particularly satisfying way.
  Describe what happens and go on to explain why you found the ending particularly satisfying.
- Choose a play that makes use of unconventional staging techniques.
  Show how the use of these techniques enables the dramatist to convey important themes to the audience.
- Choose a play that, despite being set in a specific time and place, manages to explore issues that are important to us all.
  Briefly describe the setting and go on to discuss the dramatist's exploration of these issues.

Prose

- Choose a novel or a short story in which the author creates a character for whom you develop a feeling of admiration.

  With reference to appropriate techniques, show how the author has created this character and why you admire him or her.

- Choose a novel or a short story in which the use of setting adds to the overall effectiveness of the text.

  Briefly describe the setting(s) and explain how this feature adds to the effectiveness of the text.

- Choose a novel that has a particularly satisfying ending.

  Briefly describe the ending and go on to explain how the writer's use of particular techniques makes it a satisfying one for the reader.

- Choose a novel or a short story that explores an important theme (love, death, isolation, loss, change, etc.).

  With reference to appropriate techniques, explain how the writer reveals this theme to the reader.

- Choose a novel or a short story that is set in Scotland.

  Briefly describe the setting and go on to explain why the particular setting is important to the text as a whole.

- Choose a novel or a short story in which there is a character with whom you closely identify.

  By making reference to specific literary techniques, show how the author has succeeded in making you identify with this character.

- Choose a novel or a short story that makes effective use of structure.

  Show how the writer's use of structure adds to the overall effectiveness of the text.

- Choose a novel or a short story with an unconventional hero.

  Briefly describe the unconventional aspects of this character and go on to show how they contribute to the central concerns of the text.

- Choose a novel or a short story that explores the theme of relationships.

  By making reference to specific literary techniques, show how the writer presents this theme to the reader.

- Choose a novel or a short story that seemed simple when you first read it but more complex when you read it a second time.

  By referring to specific elements of the text, show how the writer has created this complexity.

- Choose a non-fiction text that seems to teach the reader an important lesson about life.

  Briefly describe the 'lesson' and explain how the author's use of particular techniques adds to the effectiveness of his or her writing.

- Choose a non-fiction text that reveals something about the writer.

  By referring to specific techniques, show how the text does this.

- Choose a non-fiction text that deals with an important social issue in an effective way.

  By referring to specific techniques, show how the issue is presented to the reader in an effective way.

Poetry

- Choose a poem in which the form and structure chosen by the poet is particularly suited to the subject matter of the poem.

  Show how the poet has made use of form and structure to create a successful poem.

- Choose a poem that celebrates a positive aspect of life.

  Show how the poet's use of a range of poetic techniques helps to show this to the reader.

- Choose a poem that makes use of colloquial or informal language.

  Briefly say what the poem is about and go on to show how the poet's use of colloquial or informal language adds to the impact of the poem.

- Choose a poem that explores a serious theme.

  With reference to appropriate poetic techniques, show how this theme is explored in the poem.

- Choose two poems by the same poet that explore a similar theme.

  Show how the poet explores the theme in each poem and go on discuss which poem you prefer and why.

- Choose a poem in which the form and structure seem particularly suited to the subject matter.

  Briefly say what the poem is about and go on to show how the form and structure of the poem particularly suit the subject matter.

- Choose a poem in which the poet adopts a persona.

  Show how the use of a persona adds to the overall effectiveness of the text.

- Choose a poem written long ago.

  Show how, despite being written long ago, the text still has something to say to the reader of today.

- Choose a poem that deals with a powerful emotion such as love, hate, fear or anger.

  By referring to specific poetic techniques, show how the poet conveys the emotion to the reader.

- Choose a poem in which the use of sound is particularly important.

  Briefly say what the poem is about and go on to show how the poet's use of sound is particularly important to the text as a whole.

- Choose a poem that seems especially suited to a teenage reader.

  Briefly say what the poem is about and go on to explain how the poet has constructed something that appeals to this kind of audience.

Film and TV drama

- Choose a film or TV drama in which there is a main character for whom you feel dislike.

  Show how media techniques are used to portray the character in such a way that we feel dislike.

- Choose an opening scene or sequence from a film or TV drama that you consider to be particularly effective.

  Briefly describe what happens in the scene or sequence and go on to explain how the use of particular media techniques contribute to its effectiveness.

- Choose a film or TV drama that explores an issue relevant to young people today in an interesting way.

  Briefly describe the issue and then show how media techniques are used to explore it in an interesting way.

- Choose a film or TV drama that captures your interest right from the start.

  By referring to specific techniques, show how the director captures your attention in this way.

Language

- Consider the different forms of language you use depending on the situation you are in.

  By giving examples of distinctive vocabulary or grammatical constructions, show how your language changes in these different situations.
- Consider the language of advertisements for Scottish products.

  By discussing the language of one such advertisement, identify the key features that vary from other types of advertising and explain why these features could appeal to the target audience.

More study and revision advice

You'll probably spend around 4.5–5 hours in your English class each week for the National 5 course. If you are going to maximise your chances of success you need to put in a significant amount of study time over and above what you do in school.

Here are some reminders about what you should be doing throughout your course:

- If you don't understand something in class, ask your teacher at the end of the period or ask if you can speak to them at a later date – never forget that your teacher is the best resource you have.
- Make use of any study periods or dedicated revision classes offered by your school.
- Set aside some time each night (or at least Monday–Thursday) to review what you learned that day in English class.
- Write down quotations from your texts onto sticky notes and put them where you will see them regularly.
- Give yourself small tests on quotations, names of characters, techniques – anything you feel you need to remember for the exam.
- Keep a writer's notebook to jot down ideas for the pieces in your portfolio.
- Don't just make written notes – draw pictures, create diagrams or anything else that suits your learning style.
- Break down your revision into manageable sections.
- Buy cheap copies of your texts for yourself and annotate and highlight relevant content.
- Look on the internet for other resources – but ask your teacher to check if they're suitable.
- Try the following websites:
  http://www.sqa.org.uk/sqa/45674.html (the SQA's own National 5 site)
  https://secure.glowscotland.org.uk/login/login.htm (GLOW – log in with the username and password provided by your school)
  http://www.bbc.co.uk/bitesize/ (offers comprehensive notes on the Scottish texts)
  https://bubbl.us/ (a simple-to-use mind-map/revision tool)
  https://cramberry.net/ (create your own revision flashcards online)
  http://www.sparknotes.com/ (useful for revision of popular non-Scottish texts)
  http://www.shmoop.com/ (useful for revision of popular non-Scottish texts)

In addition to the tasks you do in the classroom related to the literature you are studying for the critical reading paper, it is a really good idea to make your own notes about the texts. This will encourage you to think about your own response to the writing as well as providing you with extra material to help in your revision. These notes need not be lengthy but they should be detailed enough to be helpful to you.

For novels and short stories you should make notes on:

- the structure of the story – straightforward beginning, middle, end? Flashbacks? Key scenes?
- the narrator – who is telling us the story? What are the consequences of this?
- the main characters – name, age, appearance, personality. Convincing?
- the writer's style – write down examples. Look out for techniques such as imagery and symbolism.
- the mood or atmosphere of the story
- the theme(s) – what is the writer trying to make us think about?
- your personal reaction to the text
- similarities and differences between short stories by the same writer

For drama texts you should consider:

- setting
- stage directions
- stage craft – lighting, music, sound effects
- plot structure – exposition, development, climax, key scenes, turning points
- the main characters – costume, dialogue, actions, realistic or symbolic?
- the mood or atmosphere
- the theme(s) – what issues does the playwright want the audience to think about?
- your personal reaction to the play

For poetry:
- connotations of the title
- content – what is the poem about?
- theme(s)
- poetic voice – the poet? Or a persona adopted by the poet?
- form and structure – stanza pattern, line length, metre, rhythm, rhyme
- other techniques – word choice, imagery, sentence structure
- tone
- mood
- your personal reaction to the poem

For film and TV drama:
- setting
- plot
- structure
- genre conventions – is this text typical of its kind?
- characterisation
- representation
- stereotypes
- editing
- montage
- music and sound
- special effects
- dialogue
- mise-en-scène
- camera angles
- mood or atmosphere
- your personal reaction to the film or TV drama

National 5

ENGLISH

For SQA 2019 and beyond

the education publisher
for Scotland

Practice Papers

Craig Aitchison

Introduction

National 5 English Practice Papers

This book contains two brand new and complete question papers for National 5 English, which mirror the actual SQA exam as closely as possible in question style, level, layout and appearance. It is a perfect way to familiarise yourself with the exam papers you will sit.

The answer section online at www.leckieandleckie.co.uk contains fully worked answers to each question, showing you where marks are gained in an answer and how the right answer is arrived at. It is also packed with explanatory **Hints**, which explain the answers in more detail and provide essential practical tips on tackling certain question types.

The National 5 exam is your chance to show the skills and knowledge you have acquired in reading and writing. The key to successful preparation for exams is practice. These practice exam papers will provide you with the practice you need to approach the final assessment with confidence.

The external assessment of National 5 English is divided into **Part 1: Reading for Understanding, Analysis and Evaluation** and **Part 2: Critical Reading**. Critical Reading is further divided into **Section 1: Scottish Texts** and **Section 2: Critical Essay**.

Part 1: Reading for Understanding, Analysis and Evaluation

This is the paper which in Standard Grade, Intermediate and Higher English was known as Close Reading. You will be required to read a non-fiction passage and answer questions. The passage may be a newspaper or magazine article, an extract from a piece of travel writing or biography.

The questions will cover these **three** areas:

- Showing your **understanding** of the passage by putting things in your own words, summarising and selecting key ideas.

- **Analysing** the way the writer conveys these ideas through techniques such as word choice, imagery, sentence structure and tone.

- **Evaluating** how effectively the writer conveys these ideas, giving your opinion about the writer's use of language.

Part 2: Critical Reading

Section 1: Scottish Texts

In this part of the exam you will be given an extract from the text or texts you have studied in class. This part of the paper asks you to combine **two** related skills:

1. Why is this extract important? What ideas does it present? How is language used?

2. How does the extract fit into the whole text or set of texts? For example, what themes or ideas in the extract relate to other stories or poems by the same writer?

Section 2: Critical Essay

Here you will have approximately 45 minutes to answer a question on a text you have studied in class. There will be a choice of questions covering different genres: drama, prose, poetry and film and TV drama or language study. You will be asked to focus on one aspect of your chosen text. To be able to write a well-structured, detailed answer to the question you will need to know the text fully.

This book will help you to go into the exam prepared to demonstrate your knowledge and skills. Use it for timed practice, for focused study and to guide your revision.

Practice paper A

Practice
Papers for
SQA Exams

ENGLISH

NATIONAL 5

Paper A

Reading for Understanding, Analysis and Evaluation

Duration — 1 hour

Total marks: 30

Read the extract and then answer the questions in your own words as much as possible. Try to answer all of the questions.

the education publisher
for Scotland

The world's most famous vehicle

Sometimes you don't know what you've got until it's gone.

At 9.30am on 29 January 2016, the 2,016,933rd Defender rolled off the production line at Land Rover's production line at Lode Lane, Solihull, on the outskirts of Birmingham. It marked the end of 67 years of continuous production of the world's most famous vehicle. The final Defender.

5   In all those years, the workhorse Defender had served farmers and foresters, armies and air forces, explorers and scientists, construction and utility companies – in fact, everyone who needed a good, honest vehicle that would do a good, honest job anywhere in the world. And there were a lot of people who bought one just for fun too – for its sheer brilliant off-road ability and practical attitude that made it so different to the rest of today's jelly-mould alternatives.

10 The hymn, 'Jerusalem' was sung through the factory line as generations of engineers, mechanics and factory workers paid tribute to the Land Rover Defender. This was a funereal send-off for a much-loved car that had conquered the planet. Media, journalists and film crews had descended from around the world to record this death knell. The world held its breath as the last ever Defender was driven silently out of the building.

15 This was an end that was marked by tears and sorrow, as Land Rover enthusiasts bade farewell to a familiar friend and the historic production line that had produced it fell silent.

The world mourned. This was the day the real Land Rover died.

It is said that for more than half the world's population, the first car they ever saw was a Land Rover Defender. The Defender is as British as a plate of fish and chips or a British bulldog. Like a
20 typical British person, it is stiff-upper-lipped; it never complains, and neither do we.

You climb into a Land Rover – literally; in fact, some people even need ropes to hoist themselves up into the rigid seats. The doors don't seal properly, and freezing cold rainwater, overflowing from the car's gutter (they really do have a gutter) cascades down your neck as the flimsy aluminium door invariably closes on your seat belt that dangles out of the door. The dashboard
25 consists of a series of a chunky black buttons and two analogue dials. Without heated seats, climate control options are freeze or fry. The windows always mist, even if you hold your breath. I have to pull up a metal antenna from the bonnet to pick up radio, which I can only receive while driving at 30 mph. If I crank her up to her limit of 60mph, the noise from the engine, gearbox, transfer box, differentials, tyres and the wind is deafening, and too loud to have a conversation,
30 let alone listen to anything from the speakers. There is no coffee-cup holder or hands-free. The gears grind and the seats cannot be tilted.

So, on the face of it there is not much going for the Defender. So why is it that I, along with millions of other people around the world, am so hopelessly, obsessively in love with this car?

Nothing lasts forever, but some things come close. The Defender has survived the decades largely
35 unchanged. It is a beacon of safety and security. It is favoured by the military, the police, the fire service, NGOs, the UN, the Royal Palace, the Special Forces and explorers alike. These vehicles have discovered new regions, won wars and saved lives. Across the world, the Land Rover symbolises durability and Britishness. It is estimated that three-quarters of all Land Rovers ever built are still rattling noisily across country somewhere in the world.

40 The Defender is a national treasure. We are reassured by its understated presence. It inspires a second glance but never a stare. Unshowy, unpretentious and classless, it is the car in which you can arrive at Buckingham Palace, a rural farm or an inner-city estate.

Over the years I have encountered Land Rovers in the farthest corners of the world. From steamy tropical jungles to remote islands, I have bounced across lonely landscapes in dozens, perhaps
45 hundreds of Land Rovers, many of them decades old. I have driven through the muddy trails of the Amazon basin and across the deserts of Chile in ancient Land Rovers bound together with baler twine.

When I drive through London in my Land Rover I get stopped, not for my autograph or a selfie, but for a photograph of my car. I have lost count of the number of notes slipped under the
50 windscreen wiper with offers to buy my beloved car. The children love it. The dogs love it – and so do two million other people in the world.

A vehicle that can drag a plough, clear a minefield and carry royalty, the Land Rover Defender transcends the rapidly changing world in which we live. As cars become rounder, curvier and shinier, the Land Rover Defender still looks like a child's drawing of a car, with its boxy shape. To
55 climb into a Defender is like stepping back in time to a simpler, classier world.

A Land Rover is a living breathing thing. The vehicles become characters. We name them. We learn their unique quirks. It is a sort of love affair. I know plenty of men who remember more about their old beloved Land Rovers than they do their ex-girlfriends. These cars seduce us with their charm – they are not supermodels, they are dependable, robust and loyal. There is a unique
60 relationship with a Land Rover. It is an emotional attachment like no other. How can a man-made object have such power over us?

Every Land Rover has its own unique story to tell. The world's favourite car conquered the planet and the hearts and souls of those who inhabit it … and me.

Ben Fogle, slightly adapted from the introduction to Land Rover: The Story of the Car that Conquered the World

Questions

1. Look at lines 1–4. Explain fully why these lines create an effective opening to the passage as a whole.

    3

2. Look at lines 5–20 and then explain how **two** examples of the writer's language make clear his feelings towards the Land Rover Defender.

    4

3. Look at lines 21–31 and then explain in your own words some of the flaws of the Land Rover Defender.

    4

4. Look at lines 32–33. Explain why these lines provide an appropriate link at this point in the passage.

    2

5. Look at lines 34–39. Using your own words as far as possible, explain the positive qualities of the Land Rover Defender.

    4

6. Look at lines 40–43 and then explain how **two** examples of the writer's language show how much the writer admires the Land Rover Defender.

    4

7. Look at lines 43–51. Using your own words as far as possible, explain the writer's varied experiences with Land Rovers that have led him to believe that it is a special car.

    3

8. Look at lines 52–63. Using your own words as far as possible, explain fully why the writer believes that the Land Rover is so popular.

    4

9. Look at lines 67–68. Select **one** expression from these lines and explain how it helps to make this an effective conclusion to the passage.

    2

[END OF QUESTION PAPER]

Practice Papers for SQA Exams

Duration — 1 hour and 30 minutes

Total marks: 40

Section 1: Scottish Text – 20 marks

Read an extract from a Scottish text you have previously studied.

Choose **ONE** text from either

Part A — Drama, pages 116–122

or

Part B — Prose, pages 123–132

or

Part C — Poetry, pages 133–140

Attempt **ALL** the questions for your chosen text.

Section 2: Critical Essay – 20 marks

Attempt **ONE** question from the following genres – Drama, Prose, Poetry, Film and Television Drama, or Language.

Your answer must be on a different genre from that chosen in Section 1.

You should spend approximately 45 minutes on each Section.

Write your answers clearly in the answer booklet provided. In the answer booklet you must clearly identify the question number you are attempting. Use blue or black ink. Before leaving the examination room you must give your answer booklet to the Invigilator; if you do not you may lose all the marks for this paper.

SECTION 1 — SCOTTISH TEXT — 20 marks

PART A — SCOTTISH TEXT — DRAMA

Text 1 — Drama

If you choose this text, you may not attempt a question on Drama in Section 2.

Read the extract below and then attempt the following questions. [/Question page header]

Bold Girls by Rona Munro

	MARIE:	I heard the stories. Of course I heard them.
	CASSIE:	Did you, though?
	MARIE:	He was a great-looking man. He was away a lot. There were bound to be stories.
	CASSIE:	There were books of them, Marie.
5	MARIE:	But if there'd been any truth in them Michael would've told me himself.
	CASSIE:	Oh *Marie*!
	MARIE:	That's trust Cassie!
	CASSIE:	That's *stupidity*, Marie. You haven't the sense of a hen with its head off!
	MARIE:	Michael would no more lie to me than you would, Cassie.
10	CASSIE:	Well we both did! That's what I'm telling you Marie! We were both lying to you for years!

Marie freezes where she is.

Ah Jesus … (*She moves to take another swig of her drink*)

Marie doesn't move throughout the following.

(*She can't look at Marie*) He started it but I followed it through. That was before Joe was lifted.
15 Even the smell of him was bringing my dinner up on me. I felt like I was trapped in this little black box and it was falling in on me. Michael was a window. Just a bit of excitement you know? He was exciting, Michael. . . Marie? I'm going to tell you this, Marie. I'm tired of keeping it from you. I'm tired of keeping the smile on your face. I knew it was bad. I knew lying to you was worse. I wanted to tell you. . . but I've been telling you for four years and you wouldn't hear me. Are
20 you hearing me now Marie? We'd just go out in his car, that old blue one you had before my daddy won it. Sometimes we wouldn't do anything you know? Just sit. Talk. He was a great crack, Michael. (*Pause*) I didn't think it was so bad. I always knew he loved you. He always loved you, Marie. And he did always tell you the truth, but there's only so much of the truth anyone wants to hear. That's what he gave you Marie, what he gave everyone, enough of the truth to keep us
25 all charmed.

Marie has still not moved, her eyes fixed on Cassie's face.

So. There you are. That's the truth. Now you can tear the face off me. Still nothing Marie. (*Sighing*) I'll put the kettle on.

MARIE: *(whispering)* Get out.

30 *Cassie stops.*

GET OUT OF MY HOUSE!

Cassie hesitates, she takes a step towards Marie. Marie steps back.

CASSIE: *(urgently)* Well, what did you expect? Sure, what man would tell you that kind of truth? He'd be crazy to talk about it. What woman would stand for that? If he told
35 you, he'd have to change. They'd sooner leave than they would change. Marie … you didn't want him to change.

There is a pause. Marie just stares at Cassie.

MARIE: *(whispering)* Hell isn't deep enough for you, Cassie Ryan.

Questions

1. Look at lines 1–14. In these lines, Marie refuses to believe that Michael cheated on her. Using your own words as far as possible:

   (a) Identify reasons that Marie gives for not believing. **2**

   (b) Outline Cassie's response to Marie's protests. **2**

2. Look at lines 15–29. With close reference to the text, explain what Cassie's actions and speech tell us about how she feels about her affair with Michael. You should refer to **two** examples of techniques such as word choice, tone, stage directions, etc. **4**

3. Look at lines 30–39. By referring to **two** examples, explain Marie's response to Cassie revealing the truth. You may refer to stage directions and dialogue in your answer. **4**

4. With reference to this extract and elsewhere in the play, explain the influence of male characters on the women in the play. **8**

OR

Text 2 — Drama

If you choose this text, you may not attempt a question on Drama in Section 2.

Read the extract below and then attempt the following questions.

Sailmaker **by Alan Spence**

DAVIE: Right wee religious fanatic these days eh? What is it the night then, the bandy hope?

ALEC: Christian Endeavour. Band a Hope's on Thursday.

DAVIE: Ah thought Christian Endeavour was last night?

ALEC: That was just the Juniors. Tonight's the real one.

5   DAVIE: Are ye no too young?

ALEC: The minister says ah can come.

DAVIE: Is that because ye were top in the bible exam?

ALEC: Top equal. Ah don't know if that's why. He just said ah could come.

DAVIE: Ach well, keeps ye aff the streets!

10 ALEC: Ah'll be the youngest there.

DAVIE: Mind yer heid in the door. Ye'll get stuck!

ALEC: *(Peering at himself in shaving mirror)* This wee mirror ae yours is really stupid!

DAVIE: What's up wi it?

ALEC: Look at it! There's a big crack doon the middle. The two halfs don't sit right – aw squinty.

15 DAVIE: Does me fine for shavin.

ALEC: Canny get a good look at yerself. It's dead annoyin.

DAVIE: Ach away ye go!

ALEC: Seen ma bible?

DAVIE: Try lookin where ye left it. *(ALEC looks around)* What's that under thae papers?

20 ALEC: Where?

DAVIE: There. *(Picks up book)* Naw. It's yer prize fae the Sunday School. *(Reads)* The Life of David Livingstone. Good book that. Ah read it when ah was a boy, when ah was in the Boy's Brigade. Funny, it made me want to be a missionary maself. Great White Doctor an that. Off tae darkest Africa.

25 ALEC: So what happened?

DAVIE: Och, ye know. Just … drifted away fae it. Ended up in darkest Govan instead! *(reads label in book)* Glasgow City Mission. First Prize (Equal). Bible knowledge.

ALEC: The questions were a skoosh. Who carried Christ's cross on the way to Calvary? And stuff fae the Catechism. Into what estate did the fall bring mankind? Dead easy. Just a
30   matter of rememberin.

DAVIE: Ach aye, ye take yer brains fae yer mother son. She was clever ye know. Just wurnae the same opportunities when we were young. You stick in son. Get yerself a good education. Get a decent job. Collar and tie. Never have tae take yer jacket off.

         (*Reads*) First Prize.

35   Ah was in the B.B. for a long time ye know.

         Sure and Steadfast! (*Sings*)

         Will your anchor hold

         In the storms of life

         When the clouds unfold

40   Their wings of strife

ALEC: Ah've still got yer badge for long service.

Questions

5. Look at lines 1–24.

   (a) Using your own words as far as possible, identify Davie's changing attitudes and / or feelings towards his son.   **4**

   (b) By referring to *two* examples of language, explain how the writer suggests Alec's reaction to his father.   **4**

6. Look at lines 25–41. By referring to *two* examples of language, explain how the writer makes clear the feelings that the discovery of the book brings about in Davie and Alec.   **4**

7. By referring to this extract and elsewhere in the play, show how Alec and Davie's relationship is presented.   **8**

OR

Text 3 — Drama

If you choose this text, you may not attempt a question on Drama in Section 2.

Read the extract below and then attempt the following questions.

***Tally's Blood* by Ann Marie Di Mambro**

Act 1: Scene 2

	FRANCO:	I've got a date on.
	ROSINELLA:	*(Disapproving)* Who with?
		Franco smiles, touches his nose.
	ROSINELLA:	A Scotch girl?
5		*Franco winks.*
	ROSINELLA:	I'm right, amn't I?
	FRANCO:	Could be.
	ROSINELLA:	You better watch these lassies. *(Franco scoffs)* Who is it anyway? Anybody I know?
10	FRANCO:	*(Face lights up talking about her)* This is not 'anybody'. It's Bridget Devlin. You know her?
	ROSINELLA:	*(Disapproving)* From the Auld Toon? Adam Devlin's lassie?
	FRANCO:	What if she is?
	ROSINELLA:	No harm to the lassie, Franco, but look at that family. Must be six or seven weans.
	FRANCO:	Eight.
15	ROSINELLA:	*(Shocked)* Eight weans! She keeps having them and she cannie even look after them right. And look at me! It's no fair, is it. Twelve years I've been married – and nothing. Me an Italian as well.
	FRANCO:	They're a great family, Rosinella. Really close.
	ROSINELLA:	You never met anybody in Italy?
20	FRANCO:	I wasn't looking.
	ROSINELLA:	I says to Massimo I wouldn't be surprised if you come back engaged.
	FRANCO:	I told you, Rosinella, I've got someone.
	ROSINELLA:	You're surely no keen on this Scotch girl?
	FRANCO:	What if I am?
25	ROSINELLA:	Then she must be giving you something you can't get from an Italian girl. I'm telling you, you better watch yourself.

	FRANCO:	You know nothing about Bridget.
	ROSINELLA:	Now you listen good to me, son. These Scotch girls they're all the same. They just go with you for one thing. Because your faither's got a shop and they think you've
30		got money.
	FRANCO:	*(Indignant)* Thanks very much.
	ROSINELLA:	Alright. Alright. And because you're tall …
	FRANCO:	Good-looking …
	ROSINELLA:	You're good fun to be with …
35	FRANCO:	… a good kisser, a good dancer …
	ROSINELLA:	Aye, but that's because you're Italian.
	FRANCO:	Oh, they like that alright. All I have to do is say 'Ciao Bella' and they're all over me.

Lucia in from front shop.

Ciao Bella.

40   *She jumps on his back for a piggy back.*

See what I mean?

	ROSINELLA:	Listen – these girls *(Lowers voice so Lucia won't hear)* Don't think I don't understand. You're no different from all the other Italian men. You're young, you've got the warm blood. But it's one thing to play around with them, so long as you marry
45		your own kind. You watch none of them catches you. That's the kind of thing they do here.

Questions

8. Look at lines 1–14. By referring to **two** examples, show how the writer's language helps to make clear the character of Franco. In your answer you can refer to dialogue and / or stage directions.

4

9. Look at lines 15–27. By referring to **two** examples, show how the writer's language helps to make clear the character of Rosinella.

4

10. Look at lines 28–46. By referring to **two** examples of language, show how Rosinella reveals her prejudice.

4

11. By referring to this extract and to elsewhere in the play, show how the character of Rosinella is presented.

8

PART B — SCOTTISH TEXT — PROSE

Text 1 — Prose

If you choose this text, you may not attempt a question on Prose in Section 2.

Read the extract below and then attempt the following questions.

The Cone Gatherers by Robin Jenkins

Duror had sworn that he would seize the first chance to hound them out of the wood; they were in it, he said, sore against his wish. Neil therefore had made Calum swear by an oath which he didn't understand but which to Neil was the most sacred on earth: by their dead mother, he had to swear never again to interfere with the snares. He could not remember his mother, who had
5 died soon after he was born.

Now this evening, as he trotted down the ride, he prayed by a bright star above that there would be no rabbits squealing in pain. If there were, he could not help them; he would have to rush past, tears in his eyes, fingers in his ears.

Several rabbits were caught, all dead except one; it pounded on the grass and made choking
10 noises. Neil had passed it without noticing. Calum moaned in dismay at this dilemma of either displeasing his brother or forsaking a hurt creature. He remembered his solemn promise; he remembered too the cold hatred of the gamekeeper; he knew that the penalty for interfering might be expulsion from this wood where he loved to work; but above all he shared the suffering of the rabbit.

15 When he bent down to rescue it, he had not decided in terms of right and wrong, humanity and cruelty; he had merely yielded to instinct. Accordingly he was baffled when, with one hand firmly but tenderly gripping its ears, he felt with the other to find where the wire noose held it, and discovered that both front paws were not only caught but were also broken. If he freed it, it would not be able to run; it would have to push itself along on its belly, at the mercy of its
20 many enemies. No creature on earth would help it; other rabbits would attack it because it was crippled.

As he knelt, sobbing in his quandary, the rabbit's squeals brought Neil rushing back.

'Are you daft right enough?' shouted Neil, dragging him to his feet. His voice, with its anger, sounded forlorn amidst the tall dark trees. 'Didn't you promise to leave them alone?'

25 'It's just one, Neil. Its legs are broken.'

'And what if they are? Are you such a child you're going to cry because a rabbit's legs are broken in a snare? Will you never grow up, Calum? You're a man of thirty-one, not a child of ten.'

'It's in pain, Neil.'

'Haven't I told you, hundreds of times, there's a war? Men and women and children too, at this
30 very minute, are having their legs blown away and their faces burnt off them.'

Calum whimpered.

'I ken you don't like to hear about such things, Calum. Nobody does, but they are happening, and surely they're more to worry about than a rabbit.'

'Put it out of its pain, Neil.'

35 'Am I to kill it?' In spite of him, his question was a gibe.

Calum had not the subtlety to explain why death, dealt in pity, was preferable to suffering and loneliness and ultimately death from fox's teeth or keeper's boot.

'Why don't you kill it yourself?' persisted Neil.

'I couldn't, Neil.'

40 Not only love for his brother silenced Neil then: he knew that what Calum represented, pity so meek as to be paralysed by the suffering that provoked it, ought to be regretted perhaps, but never despised.

Questions

12. Look at lines 1–8. Using your own words as far as possible, explain the reasons why Calum decides he has to 'rush past' this part of the wood.

2

13. Look at lines 9–21. By referring to **two** examples of language, explain how the writer makes clear Calum's feelings when he discovers the rabbit caught in the snare.

4

14. Look at lines 22–39. By referring to **two** examples of language, explain how the writer makes clear Neil's reaction to Calum's behaviour.

4

15. Look at lines 40–42. Explain, using your own words as far as possible, Neil's change in attitude in these lines.

2

16. With reference to this extract and elsewhere in the novel, explain how the theme of nature is explored.

8

OR

Text 2 — Prose

If you choose this text, you may not attempt a question on Prose in Section 2.

Read the extract below and then attempt the following questions.

The Testament of Gideon Mack by James Robertson

This extract describes the moment that Gideon falls into the Black Jaws.

I remember this: I fell into a roaring mouth that instantly became a cold, wet, hard throat sucking me down and down into itself. Nobody but I know how apt the name *the Black Jaws* is for that dreadful place, for nobody else has been devoured by it and lived. I fell, as helpless as the rabbit that had gone before me, and at some point all my senses were smothered in the darkness. I
5   don't know when this happened, whether I was still in the air or had hit the water, but I have no memory of hitting the water. The last thing I remember thinking was the mundane fact that I had eaten nothing since breakfast.

Then there was a tremendous, freezing pressure all around me, and I was being churned and spun like a sock in a washing-machine, carried along by an immense, frothing, surging force.
10   Something hit me, or I hit it. I was caught for a second, snagged, then I was moving again. This is all I can remember of however long I was in the Black Jaws.

Somewhere in my head was the knowledge that I couldn't possibly have survived the fall; that even if I had, the river would have killed me; drowned, broken, battered, chilled and crushed me to pulp. I was of the opinion, therefore, that I must be dead.

15   And yet I remained in the body that had been Gideon Mack. It was as if the essence of me was trapped in that now useless shell, that rudderless vessel spinning like a barrel in the flood. I was moving very rapidly in black water through a long black tunnel. My head kept going under, coming up again. I tried to breathe, but there was no room for breath in my lungs. The tunnel must have been dimly lit because I could see the black rock of its roof and walls, and the horrible,
20   sickly race of the water rushing me along. I tried to see where the light was coming from. I couldn't possibly swim in such a current, but as I travelled I was turned by it and whenever I was facing in the direction of the flow I saw a tiny speck of yellow not far in the distance. This was the light that cast just enough of itself to illuminate the tunnel, and I was moving towards it. The tunnel was very straight, the river more like a mill-lade than a natural river. I felt that I was being
25   propelled along at hundreds of miles per hour.

And yet I did not panic. There was no point in panicking. I could do nothing. Everything was out of my hands. I could only be taken by the water wherever it was going. The water was very cold and did not seem quite real, it was thick and viscous yet at the same time it flowed as freely as a burn; it was both solid and liquid at the same time. And it was carrying me towards the light.

30   The light grew brighter. My sense of calmness grew with it. I did not want to be calm, I felt I ought to be fighting for my life – but at the same time I thought I was dead. And as this thought intensified, become a certainty, in some indefinite moment the essence of me slipped away from my physical self. And my consciousness was with the essence. I was the kite I had flown in the

garden, centuries before it seemed, attached but at a distance, outside, above, looking down
35 on my body as it was swept along the tunnel. I was hovering above it, keeping pace and yet
not moving at all. I had a memory of watching myself on the bedroom floor all those years
before, the sounds of Jenny working in the kitchen below. Then I had other memories: Elsie
and me in that same bedroom making love, me and Buzz arguing in the school playground
with part of me outside looking on, John and me identifying Jenny at the hospital, my mother
40 watching me sleepwalking, my father's vicelike grip on my neck in front of the television, my
mother kneeling beside my father on the floor, the little pile of yellow vomit at his mouth.
These and other images appeared as if I was looking at them in a flicker-book. I thought, *this is
a ridiculous cliché, my life is flashing in front of me*, but it was true and I could not stop it. And all
the while the light was growing brighter.

Questions

17. Look at lines 1–12. By referring to **two** examples of language, explain how the writer
makes the Black Jaws seem terrifying.   **4**

18. Look at lines 16–26. Using your own words as far as possible, explain Gideon's experience
in the tunnel.   **4**

19. Look at lines 27–45. By referring to **two** examples of language from these lines, explain
how the writer makes Gideon's feelings clear.   **4**

20. Referring to this extract and elsewhere in the novel, show how the theme of belief is
explored.   **8**

OR

Text 3 — Prose

If you choose this text, you may not attempt a question on Prose in Section 2.

Read the extract below and then attempt the following questions.

The Strange Case of Dr Jekyll and Mr Hyde by Robert Louis Stevenson

Nearly a year later, in the month of October, 18—, London was startled by a crime of singular ferocity and rendered all the more notable by the high position of the victim. The details were few and startling. A maid servant living alone in a house not far from the river, had gone upstairs to bed about eleven. Although a fog rolled over the city in the small hours, the early part of
5 the night was cloudless, and the lane, which the maid's window overlooked, was brilliantly lit by the full moon. It seems she was romantically given, for she sat down upon her box, which stood immediately under the window, and fell into a dream of musing. Never (she used to say, with streaming tears, when she narrated that experience), never had she felt more at peace with all men or thought more kindly of the world. And as she so sat she became aware of an
10 aged beautiful gentleman with white hair, drawing near along the lane; and advancing to meet him, another and very small gentleman, to whom at first she paid less attention. When they had come within speech (which was just under the maid's eyes) the older man bowed and accosted the other with a very pretty manner of politeness. It did not seem as if the subject of his address were of great importance; indeed, from his pointing, it some times appeared as if
15 he were only inquiring his way; but the moon shone on his face as he spoke, and the girl was pleased to watch it, it seemed to breathe such an innocent and old-world kindness of disposition, yet with something high too, as of a well-founded self-content. Presently her eye wandered to the other, and she was surprised to recognise in him a certain Mr. Hyde, who had once visited her master and for whom she had conceived a dislike. He had in his hand a heavy cane, with
20 which he was trifling; but he answered never a word, and seemed to listen with an ill-contained impatience. And then all of a sudden he broke out in a great flame of anger, stamping with his foot, brandishing the cane, and carrying on (as the maid described it) like a madman. The old gentleman took a step back, with the air of one very much surprised and a trifle hurt; and at that Mr. Hyde broke out of all bounds and clubbed him to the earth. And next moment, with ape-like
25 fury, he was trampling his victim under foot and hailing down a storm of blows, under which the bones were audibly shattered and the body jumped upon the roadway. At the horror of these sights and sounds, the maid fainted.

It was two o'clock when she came to herself and called for the police. The murderer was gone long ago; but there lay his victim in the middle of the lane, incredibly mangled. The stick with
30 which the deed had been done, although it was of some rare and very tough and heavy wood, had broken in the middle under the stress of this insensate cruelty; and one splintered half had rolled in the neighbouring gutter—the other, without doubt, had been carried away by the murderer. A purse and gold watch were found upon the victim: but no cards or papers, except a sealed and stamped envelope, which he had been probably carrying to the post, and which bore
35 the name and address of Mr. Utterson.

Questions

21. Using your own words as far as possible, summarise the maid's experience as described in this extract. Make **four** clear points.

    4

22. Look at lines 1–17 ('Nearly a year later … self-content.'). Explain how the writer's use of language makes clear the character of:

    (a) The maid

    2

    (b) Hyde's victim

    2

23. Look at lines 18–35 ('Presently her eye … Mr. Utterson.'). Explain how **two** examples of the writer's use of language contribute to our understanding of the character of Mr Hyde.

    4

24. By referring to this extract and to elsewhere in the novel, describe the theme of good versus evil throughout the novel.

    8

OR

Text 4 — Prose

If you choose this text, you may not attempt a question on Prose in Section 2.

Read the extract below and then attempt the following questions.

Home by Iain Crichton Smith

'What would the Bruces say if they saw you running about in this dirty place like a schoolboy?' she said coldly.

'What dae ye mean?'

'Simply what I said. There was no need to come here at all. Or do you want to take a photograph
5 and show it to them? "The Place Where I Was Born".'

'I wasna born here. I just lived here for five years.'

'What would they think of you, I wonder.'

'I don't give a damn about the Bruces,' he burst out, the veins on his forehead swelling. 'What's
he but a doctor anyway? I'm not ashamed of it. And, by God, why should you be ashamed of
10 it? You weren't brought up in a fine house either. You worked in a factory till I picked you up at
that dance.'

She turned away.

'Do you mind that night?' he asked contritely. 'You were standing by the wall and I went up to you
and I said, "Could I have the honour?" And when we were coming home we walked down lovers'
15 lane, where they had all the seats and the statues.'

'And you made a clown of yourself,' she said unforgivingly.

'Yes, didn't I just?' remembering how he had climbed the statue in the moonlight to show off.
From the top of it he could see the Clyde, the ships and the cranes.

'And remember the flicks?' he said. 'We used tae get in wi jam jars. And do you mind the man who
20 used to come down the passage at interval spraying us with disinfectant?'

The interior of the cinema came back to him in a warm flood: the children in the front rows
keeping up a continual barrage of noise, the ushers hushing them, the smoke, the warmth, the
pies slapping against faces, the carved cherubs in the flaking roof blowing their trumpets.

'You'd like that, wouldn't you?' she said. 'Remember it was me who drove you to the top.'

25 'Whit dae ye mean?' – like a bull wounded in the arena.

'You were lazy, that was what was wrong with you. You'd go out ferreting when you were here.
You liked being with the boys.'

'Nothing wrong with that. What's wrong wi that?'

'What do you want? That they should all wave flags? That all the dirty boys and girls should
30 line the street with banners five miles high? They don't give a damn about you, you know that.
They're all dead and rotting and we should be back in Africa where we belong.'

He heard the voices round him. It was New Year's Eve and they were all dancing in a restaurant
which had a fountain in the middle, and in the basin hundreds of pennies.

'Knees up, Mother Brown,' Jamieson was shouting to Hannah.

35 'You used to dance, too,' he said, 'on New Year's Night.'

'I saw old Manson dying in that room,' he said, pointing at a window. The floor and the ceiling
and the walls seemed to have drops of perspiration and Manson had a brown flannel cloth
wrapped round his neck. He couldn't breathe. And he heard the mice scuttering behind
the walls.

40 She turned on him. 'What are you bringing that up for? Why don't you forget it? Do you enjoy
thinking about these things?'

'Shut up,' he shouted, 'you didn't even have proper table manners when I met you.'

She stalked out to the car and he stayed where he was. To hell with her. She couldn't drive
anyway.

Questions

25. Using your own words as far as possible, identify the key things that cause tension
between the man and his wife. You should make **four** key points in your answer.   **4**

26. Look at lines 1–25. By referring to **two** examples, explain how the writer's use of language
makes clear the man's changing emotions.   **4**

27. Look at lines 26–40. By referring to **two** examples, explain how the writer's use of
language makes clear his wife's feelings.   **4**

28. By referring to this extract and to at least **one** other story by Crichton Smith, show how a
sense of place is important to his stories.   **8**

OR

Text 5 — Prose

If you choose this text, you may not attempt a question on Prose in Section 2.

Read the extract below and then attempt the following questions.

Hieroglyphics **by Anne Donovan**

Do you know what heiroglyphics are, Mary?

Aye sur. It's Egyptian writing.

Yes, sir, not Aye, sir. I is the first person nominative, not that any of you will know what that means of course, since you no longer have the good fortune to be properly educated in the classical

5 tradition. Maybe if you would learn to speak properly you could then write properly.

The class were aw sittin up like circus lions at this point, wonderin whit the ringmaister wis gonny dae next. Sometimes he would launch intae a big long speech and then ye didnae huv tae dae oany work. Which wis hunky dory as long as you wereny the wan he'd lamped oanty.

So, Mary, if hieroglyphics means Egyptian writing, why do you think I am referring to your script

10 using that term?

Because you canny ... can't read it, Sir.

Precisely Mary. And since the function of reading is to communicate, what point is there in writing something which is utterly unintelligible?

Ah jist sat there.

15 Well, Mary, I'm awaiting your answer.

But if you were an Egyptian you could read hieroglyphics, sur.

Are you trying to be funny, girl?

No sur.

I thought not. Well, Mary, since neither you nor I nor anyone in this room appears to hail from

20 ancient Egypt, you are going to have to learn to write in a legible hand. And since you have not managed to write down today's notes then I suggest you borrow someone else's jotter and copy them out tonight.

Ah wis mortified, pure mortified. The lassie next tae me passed her jotter ower wioot sayin a word and ah pit it in ma bag and walked oot the room. And from that day sumpn funny startit tae

25 happen that ah couldnae unnerstaun. The class stopped talkin tae me but it wisnae like they'd aw fell oot wi me; ah mean if ah asked tae borrow their tippex or said did ye see Home and Away last night they wid answer me, but they widnae say much and they never startit a conversation wi me. And there seemed tae be an empty space aw roond me in the class, fur naebdy sat next tae me if they could help it. Ah couldnae figure it oot, fur they aw hatit auld Skelly, so how come jist

30 because he didnae like me they didnae either. You'd hink it wid be the ither way roond.

And it wisnae jist in his class either, ah could of unnerstood that aw right fur who wants tae sit near the target practice? But it wis in every class, and the playgrund and the dinner school. And when ye move up tae the big school it's a time when friendships kindy shuffle roond like wanny they progressive barn dances, and ye make new wans an ye lose auld wans and
35   somehow in the middly aw this process ah fund masel oot the dance wioot a partner. And it wisnae nice.

Then ah startit daein the hieroglyphics fur real. In the beginnin it wis part of oor History project on the Egyptians. We aw hud tae make up oor ain version, writin wee messages and stories. Miss Niven presented it tae us as if it wis some crackin new original idea though of
40   course we done it in Primary Four (but we didnae tell her that cos it wis better than readin aboot the preservation a mummies). And ah turnt oot tae be dead good at it. Somehow the wee pictures jist seemed tae come intae ma heid and it wis that easy compared tae writin words. If ye wanted tae say would you like a cup of tea? ye jist drew a wee cupnsaucer an a mooth wi an arra pointin at it and a question mark. Nae worryin aboot whit kindy wood it wis
45   or how many e's in tea.

Questions

29. Using your own words as far as possible, identify **four** things we learn about Mary's experiences at school.   **4**

30. Look at lines 1–22. By referring to **two** examples, explain how the writer's use of language makes clear Mr Skelly's attitude to Mary.   **4**

31. Look at lines 23–46. By referring to **two** examples, explain how the writer's use of language makes clear Mary's feelings about the way the other pupils treat her.   **4**

32. By referring to this extract and to at least **one** other story by Donovan, show how she presents the idea of communication.   **8**

PART C — SCOTTISH TEXT — POETRY

Text 1 — Poetry

If you choose this text, you may not attempt a question on Poetry in Section 2.

Read the poem below and then attempt the following questions.

***In Mrs Tilscher's Class* by Carol Ann Duffy**

You could travel up the Blue Nile
with your finger, tracing the route
while Mrs Tilscher chanted the scenery
Tana. Ethiopia. Khartoum. Aswan.
5 That for an hour, then a skittle of milk
and the chalky Pyramids rubbed into dust.
A window opened with a long pole.
The laugh of a bell swung by a running child.

This was better than home. Enthralling books.
10 The classroom glowed like a sweetshop.
Sugar paper. Coloured shapes. Brady and Hindley
faded, like a faint uneasy smudge of a mistake.
Mrs Tilscher loved you. Some mornings, you found
she'd left a good gold star by your name.
15 The scent of a pencil, slowly, carefully, shaved.
A xylophone's nonsense heard from another form.

Over the Easter term, the inky tadpoles changed
from commas into exclamation marks. Three frogs
hopped in the playground, freed by a dunce,
20 followed by a line of kids, jumping and croaking
away from the lunch queue. A rough boy
told you how you were born. You kicked him, but stared
at your parents, appalled, when you got back home.

That feverish July, the air tasted of electricity.
25 A tangible alarm made you always untidy, hot,
fractious under the heavy sexy sky. You asked her
how you were born and Mrs Tilscher smiled,
then turned away. Reports were handed out.
You ran through the gates, impatient to be grown,
30 As the sky split open into a thunderstorm.

Questions

33. Look at lines 1–16. By referring to **two** examples of language, explain how the writer's use of language creates a clear impression of how the child felt about school.

4

34. Look at lines 17–23. By referring to **two** examples of language, explain how the writer's use of language creates a sense of change.

4

35. Look at lines 24–30. By referring to **two** examples of language, explain how the writer's use of language creates a clear understanding of the child's discomfort.

4

36. By referring to this poem and to at least **one** other poem by Duffy, show how she presents the idea of change.

8

OR

Text 2 — Poetry

If you choose this text, you may not attempt a question on Poetry in Section 2.

Read the poem below and then attempt the following questions.

Glasgow 5th March 1971 **by Edwin Morgan**

With a ragged diamond

of shattered plate-glass

a young man and his girl

are falling backwards into a shop-window.

5   The young man's face

is bristling with fragments of glass

and the girl's leg has caught

on the broken window

and spurts arterial blood

10   over her wet-look white coat.

Their arms are starfished out

braced for impact.

Their faces show surprise, shock,

and the beginning of pain.

15   The two youths who have pushed them

are about to complete the operation

reaching into the window

to loot what they can smartly.

Their faces show no expression.

20   It is a sharp clear night

in Sauchiehall Street.

In the background two drivers

keep their eyes on the road.

Questions

37. Look at lines 1–4. By referring to **one** example of language, explain how the poet creates an attention-grabbing opening to the poem.

2

38. Look at lines 5–14. By referring to **two** examples of language, explain how the poet's word choice makes clear the violence of the incident described.

4

39. Look at lines 15–19. By referring to **two** examples of language, explain how the poet creates a strong impression of the 'youths' that committed the crime.

4

40. Look at lines 20–23. How effective do you find these lines as a conclusion to the poem? You should refer to **one** example from these lines, and to the language and / or ideas of the rest of the poem.

2

41. By referring to this poem and to at least **one** other by Morgan, show how he deals with themes that are important to modern society.

8

OR

Text 3 — Poetry

If you choose this text, you may not attempt a question on Poetry in Section 2.

Read the poem below and then attempt the following questions.

***Brooklyn Cop* by Norman MacCaig**

Built like a gorilla but less timid,
thickfleshed, steakcoloured, with two
hieroglyphs in his face that mean
trouble, he walks the sidewalk and the
5   thin tissue over violence. This morning,
when he said, "See you, babe" to his wife,
he hoped it, he truly hoped it.
He is a gorilla
to whom "Hiya, honey" is no cliché.

10 Should the tissue tear, should he plunge through
into violence, what clubbings, what
gunshots between Phoebe's Whamburger
and Louie's Place.

Who would be him, gorilla with a nightstick,
15 whose home is a place
he might, this time, never get back to?

And who would be who have to be
his victims?

Questions

42. Look at lines 1–7. By referring to **three** examples of language, explain how the poet creates a clear impression of the cop's life and personality.

6

43. Look at lines 10–13. By referring to **two** examples of language, explain how the poet creates a clear impression of the world the cop inhabits.

4

44. Look at lines 14–18. By referring to **one** example of language, explain how the poet creates an emotional response in the reader.

2

45. By referring to this poem and to at least **one** other by MacCaig, show how he uses poetry to confront the darker side of human experience.

8

OR

Text 4 — Poetry

If you choose this text, you may not attempt a question on Poetry in Section 2.

Read the poem below and then attempt the following questions.

***Old Tongue* by Jackie Kay**

When I was eight, I was forced south.
Not long after, when I opened
my mouth, a strange thing happened.
I lost my Scottish accent.
5 Words fell off my tongue:
eedyit, dreich, wabbit, crabbit,
stummer, teuchter, heidbanger,
so you are, so am ur, see you, see ma ma,
shut yer geggie, or I'll gie you the malkie!

10 My own vowels started to stretch like my bones
and I turned my back on Scotland.
Words disappeared in the dead of night,
new words marched in: ghastly, awful,
quite dreadful, scones said like stones.
15 Pokey hats into ice-cream cones.
Oh where did all my words go –
my old words, my lost words?
Did you ever feel sad when you lost a word,
did you ever try and call it back
20 like calling in the sea?
If I could have found my words wandering,
I swear I would have taken them in,
swallowed them whole, knocked them back.

Out in the English soil, my old words
25 buried themselves. It made my mother's blood boil.
I cried one day with the wrong sound in my mouth.
I wanted them back; I wanted my old accent back,
my old tongue. My dour, soor Scottish tongue.
Sing-songy. I wanted to gie it laldie.

Questions

46. Look at lines 1–15. By referring to **two** examples of language, explain how the poet makes clear her emotions.

4

47. Look at lines 16–25. By referring to **two** examples of language, explain how the poet makes clear her feelings in these lines.

4

48. Look at lines 26–29. By referring to **two** examples of language, explain how these lines show how strongly the poet feels about the change in the way that she speaks.

4

49. By referring to this poem and to at least **one** other by Kay, show how she explores the theme of change.

8

SECTION 2 — CRITICAL ESSAY — 20 marks

Attempt ONE question from the following genres — Drama, Prose, Poetry, Film and Television Drama, or Language. Your answer must be on a different genre from that chosen in Section 1. You should spend approximately 45 minutes on this Section.

DRAMA

> *Answers to questions in this part should refer to the text and to such relevant features as characterisation, key scene(s), structure, climax, theme, plot, conflict, setting …*

1. Choose a play in which a character changes or develops.

   Describe how the character changes with reference to the playwright's use of dramatic techniques.

2. Choose a play in which there is a scene that produces strong emotions in the audience.

   Briefly describe what happens in this scene, and by referring to appropriate dramatic techniques, go on to explain why the scene is important to the play as a whole.

PROSE

> *Answers to questions in this part should refer to the text and to such relevant features as characterisation, setting, language, key incident(s), climax, turning point, plot, structure, narrative technique, theme, ideas, description …*

3. Choose a novel or a short story or a work of non-fiction that has an emotional impact on the reader.

   By referring to appropriate techniques, show how the writer achieves this emotional impact.

4. Choose a novel or a short story that has an interesting relationship between characters.

   By referring to appropriate techniques, show how the writer makes this relationship interesting.

POETRY

> *Answers to questions in this part should refer to the text and to such relevant features as word choice, tone, imagery, structure, content, rhythm, rhyme, theme, sound, ideas …*

5. Choose a poem that describes a significant moment.

   By referring to poetic techniques, explain how the significance of this moment is conveyed by the poet.

6. Choose a poem that describes a person or place in detail.

   By referring to poetic techniques, explain how and why the poet describes this person or place.

FILM AND TELEVISION DRAMA*

Answers to questions in this part should refer to the text and to such relevant features as use of camera, key sequence, characterisation, mise-en-scène, editing, setting, music / sound, special effects, plot, dialogue …

7. Choose a scene or a sequence from a film or TV drama that creates a strong emotion in the audience.

   Explain what this emotion is and by referring to appropriate techniques, explain how these emotions are evoked.

8. Choose a film or TV drama that explores an important issue.

   By referring to appropriate techniques, explain how the director presents the issue in the film / TV drama as a whole.

* 'TV drama' includes a single play, a series or a serial.

LANGUAGE

Answers to questions in this part should refer to the text and to such relevant features as register, accent, dialect, slang, jargon, vocabulary, tone, abbreviation …

9. Choose an advertisement that uses language particularly effectively.

   By referring to specific examples from the advertisement, explain why the language used was particularly effective.

10. Consider the language used by a specific group of people who are linked in some way such as their age, job, interests.

    By referring to specific examples, explain how the language of this group is different from the language used by the general population.

[END OF QUESTION PAPER]

Practice paper B

Practice paper B

Practice Papers for SQA Exams

ENGLISH

NATIONAL 5

Paper B

Reading for Understanding, Analysis and Evaluation

Duration — 1 hour

Total marks: 30

Read the extract and then answer the questions in your own words as much as possible. Try to answer all of the questions.

the education publisher

for Scotland

Diversify

The British writer EM Forster famously wrote 'Only connect.'

And he was absolutely right. While the Earth is vast, we live in a small world full of opportunities to connect with each other, and it's only when we do this that the walls between us come down. Yet the majority of us seem to find this incredibly difficult, caught up as we are in the things that
5   divide us.

In one sense, of course, we are more connected than we've ever been before. Whether we live in the remotest parts of the world or in great international cities such as London or New York, we can connect across the globe at the click of a button. So it's a great irony that the economic gap between those at the centre of society and those at the periphery is ever-growing. Our great
10   cities of culture and commerce are in fact cities of strangers, where individuals have rejected relationships with neighbours in favour of superficial relationships with an online community. We often ignore passersby as we get on with our lives. We continue on, unaffected by what happens to 'others.'

And yet, we have far more in common than that which divides us. This is scientific fact.
15   Genetically, human beings are 99.9 per cent identical. Our bodies perform in the same way – we breathe the same, we eat the same, we sleep the same – and yet we choose to focus so much on the 0.1 per cent that makes us different – the 0.1 that determines external physical attributes such as hair, eye and skin colour.

This focus has been the cause of so much tension and strife in the world, yet by re-evaluating
20   the importance we place on it, we have the power to change how it affects our future. What if we celebrated that 0.1 per cent rather than feared it? What amazing things might follow for our society? The need to do this has never been so urgent.

We are now more divided than ever before – but the ability to change this is firmly within our grasp. We need to diversify, and we need to do it now. This is an issue I've felt passionate about for
25   a long time: it informs my work, my relationships and my everyday life.

In 2008 I moved to the US and started working in American TV. One day, when I was filming in Las Vegas, a young sound assistant appeared on set. I noticed him straight away – and immediately felt uneasy around him. He hadn't behaved aggressively towards me, but he was covered in tattoos. And I'm not talking David Beckham-style ink, but rather what looked like gang markings.
30   I suspected he'd probably had a tough upbringing, possibly had a few run-ins with the law in his time. But had I really just painted this picture and gained this insight into another person's life based on some tattoos and a bad ponytail? Yes, I had. And, regardless of the illogic of my assumptions, I began to feel intimidated.

As a woman of colour, I am all too aware of the problems that can be caused by stereotyping.
35   In fact, being excluded as a result of being a woman, and being excluded because of your race, are two forms of discrimination I understand first-hand. So you might think that I, of all people, should know better, and should get over my discomfort and preconceived ideas and just have a conversation with this man. But in that moment I couldn't do it.

40 I was about to quietly exclude this young man. Basically, I was prepared to pretend he wasn't there so I could feel comfortable.

But I'm happy to say that I didn't. In that light-bulb moment, I chose to be my better self and to challenge some of my own limiting beliefs. Limiting beliefs that I didn't even realise I had. So I went over nervously and did what usually comes very naturally to me: I spoke to him.

As it happens, he had indeed had a difficult start in life. However, he had also done a great deal of
45 studying and self-development, and was now committed to making a better life for himself and was extremely excited about the possibility of a career as a sound-man. He was brimming with enthusiasm and full of dreams – dreams that, I sensed, he secretly hoped wouldn't be dashed by those prejudging him. Fortunately, our lead soundman had looked beyond his exterior and taken him on as an apprentice, but I couldn't help but lament what it would take for him to rise above
50 the limiting beliefs of others in order to achieve his full potential. He was a truly gentle soul, yet I could sense the unspoken burden he had to carry because of his appearance and the effect it had on people like me – he had to go out of his way to seem unthreatening, and to overcompensate with helpfulness.

I ended up having one of the most enlightening conversations of my life with this young man –
55 and I realised that, had I not been able to put aside my issues around his appearance, I would have missed out on a defining moment that not only changed the way I think, but also enabled me to truly understand both sides of a problem that affects me personally. It made me wonder how many of us miss out on enriching, enlightening, even magical moments every day due to our failure to put aside our issues with external packaging.

60 I still have a funny feeling in my stomach every time I tell this story, because to own the positive outcome, I have to accept that I went into the situation with prejudice. And this is not who I consider myself to be. But this belief itself is limited, because we are all hardwired with stereotypes – perceptions of what looks like safety and comfort, and what looks unfamiliar, something to be kept out. At times these ideas protect us, but they often trap us, too.
65 Stereotypical assumptions on who should lead and who should follow limit potential, which in turn limits us all. Those to whom we mentally close our gates may well possess the answers to some of the greatest challenge of our age: extremism, economic instability, poverty, and the sustainability of the planet itself. To solve these complex problems (which don't appear to be going anywhere), we need to nurture the greatest minds of our age – whatever body they
70 reside in.

June Sarpong, adapted from the introduction to Diversify

Questions

1. Look at lines 1–5 and, using your own words as far as possible, identify **two** of the writer's beliefs.

    2

2. Look at lines 6–13. Using your own words as far as possible, explain the contradiction described in these lines.

    2

3. Look at lines 14–18.

    (a) Explain why the sentence, 'And yet … divides us.' provides an effective link at this point in the passage.

    2

    (b) Using your own words as far as possible, explain why the writer believes we 'have far more in common than that which divides us.'

    2

4. Look at lines 19–25. By referring to **two** examples of language, show how the writer emphasises the idea that we should connect. In your answer you should refer to both word choice **and** sentence structure.

    4

5. Look at lines 26–33. Using your own words as far as possible, identify reasons why the sound assistant made the writer feel 'uneasy'.

    2

6. Look at lines 34–40. Using your own words as far as possible, explain the dilemma the writer describes in these lines.

    4

7. Look at lines 41–43. Explain fully why the metaphor 'light-bulb moment' (line 41) is effective here.

    2

8. Look at lines 44–53. Using your own words as far as possible, explain what the writer learned about the young man.

    4

9. Look at lines 54–59. Identify, in your own words as far as possible, the impact of this conversation on the writer.

    2

10. Look at lines 60–70. Select any **two** expressions from these lines and explain how they contribute to the passage's effective conclusion.

    4

[END OF QUESTION PAPER]

N5 Practice Papers for SQA Exams

ENGLISH
NATIONAL 5
Paper B
Critical Reading

Duration — 1 hour and 30 minutes

Total marks: 40

Section 1: Scottish Text – 20 marks

Read an extract from a Scottish text you have previously studied.

Choose **ONE** text from either

Part A — Drama, pages 150–155

or

Part B — Prose, pages 156–165

or

Part C — Poetry, pages 166–173

Attempt **ALL** the questions for your chosen text.

Section 2: Critical Essay – 20 marks

Attempt **ONE** question from the following genres — Drama, Prose, Poetry, Film and Television Drama, or Language.

Your answer must be on a different genre from that chosen in Section 1.

You should spend approximately 45 minutes on each Section.

Write your answers clearly in the answer booklet provided. In the answer booklet you must clearly identify the question number you are attempting. Use blue or black ink. Before leaving the examination room you must give your answer booklet to the Invigilator; if you do not you may lose all the marks for this paper.

SECTION 1 — SCOTTISH TEXT — 20 marks

PART A — SCOTTISH TEXT — DRAMA

Text 1 — Drama

If you choose this text, you may not attempt a question on Drama in Section 2.

Read the extract below and then attempt the following questions.

Bold Girls by Rona Munro

Marie comes back into the room and starts two jobs simultaneously. First she puts the crisps etc. away, then she fills a pan with water and throws it on the stove. She starts sorting her dry washing into what needs ironing and what doesn't; she sorts a few items then starts peeling potatoes; all her movements have a frenetic efficiency. Nora enters with a pile of damp sheets. She is down-to-earth, middle-aged.

5	NORA:	Is that the last of them, Marie?
	MARIE:	Just the towels … Oh Nora, you didn't need to carry that over, wee Michael was coming to get them.
	NORA:	Och you're all right. These towels is it?
	MARIE:	That's them.
10	NORA:	This'll need to be the last. I've a load of my own to get in.
	MARIE:	Oh here Nora, leave them then!
	NORA:	No, no, we're best all getting our wash done while it's dry. We'll wait long enough to see the sun again.
	CASSIE:	Can I ask you a personal question, Marie?
15	NORA:	Have you left that machine on, Cassie?
	CASSIE:	Do you have a pair of red knickers?
	MARIE:	I think I do, yes.
	CASSIE:	With wee black cats, with wee balloons coming out their mouths saying 'Hug me, I'm cuddly'?
20	MARIE:	*(stops peeling potatoes briefly; giving Cassie a severe look)* They were in a pack of three for ninety-nine pence.
	NORA:	You see if you leave it, it just boils over, you know that Cassie.
	CASSIE:	And did you put those knickers in the wash you just gave my mother?
	NORA:	It's because that powder isn't really biological, it's something else altogether.
25	MARIE:	What's happened to them?
	NORA:	I think it's for dishwashers. But it was in bulk, cheap you know? I got a load of it at the club last month, awful nice young man, do you know that Dooley boy?

CASSIE: And did my mummy just drop those bright red knickers with their wee cats, right in
            the middle of the road, right by the ice cream van, as she was coming across from
30   our house to yours?

NORA: Did I what?

MARIE: Oh no! *(She increases the pace of her peeling)*

NORA: Cassie, will you get back over the road and see to that machine before the foam's
            coming down the steps to greet us.

35 MARIE: Where are they?

CASSIE: At the top of the lamp-post. I didn't know wee Colm could climb like that, he's only
            nine.

NORA: Och I'll do it myself. *(She moves to exit with a heap of towels)*

MARIE: Hold on Nora, I'm coming too.

40 CASSIE: I wouldn't. After what's been said about those knickers I'd just leave them alone,
            pretend you never saw them in your life.

Questions

1. Look at the stage directions in lines 1–4. Using your own words as far as possible, identify
   what we find out about Marie's character from these stage directions.   **2**

2. Look at lines 5–27. Explain what the language of these lines reveals about the character of
   Nora and / or Marie and / or Cassie.   **6**

3. Look at lines 28–40. Explain how **two** examples of the language of these lines creates
   humour.   **4**

4. By referring to this extract, and to elsewhere in the play, explain how the writer portrays
   the theme of female relationships.   **8**

OR

Text 2 — Drama

If you choose this text, you may not attempt a question on Drama in Section 2.

Read the extract below and then attempt the following questions.

Sailmaker by Alan Spence

ALEC: Ah've been thinkin da. When ah go tae the University ah might get a wee place ae ma own. Wee bedsit or somethin. Over near the Uni.

DAVIE: Oh aye. Will that no be dear?

ALEC: Shouldnae be too bad.

5   DAVIE: Whatever ye think.

ALEC: Ah'll see what happens.

DAVIE: Aye. (*Silence between them. DAVIE takes up tools*) These are made fae lignum vitae.

ALEC: That's Latin. Wood of life.

DAVIE: Hardest wood in the world. Should burn nice an slow. (*Puts in fire*) Thae other tools can
10   go in the midden sometime. (*Watches fire*) Is there anythin else?

ALEC: There's this. (*Indicates chair*)

DAVIE: This is part of the furniture we got when we were married. Got it in Galpern's. That's him that was the Lord Provost. Solid stuff it is too. Nobody takes the care any more. Nobody's interested in this auld stuff. (*He is talking himself into being sad*)

15   Ah remember when we bought it. Seems a shame tae break it up. Still it's a shame tae freeze as well, isn't it. (*Breaks up chair, they watch it burn*)

ALEC: (*Picks up yacht*) That just leaves this.

DAVIE: Yer Uncle Billy painted it.

ALEC: You were always gonnae fix it up for me. Ah could always imagine it. Like that song. Red
20   sails in the sunset.

DAVIE: Ah always meant to. Just …

ALEC: Just never did.

DAVIE: Story a ma life.

ALEC: (*Comes forward with yacht*) When the last bit of furniture had burned down, I wedged
25   the yacht in the grate.

The flames licked round it.

The paint began to blister and bubble.

Then the wood of the hull caught and burned.

And the yacht had a sail of flame.

30 And it sailed in the fire, like a Viking longboat, out to sea in a blaze with the body of a dead chief.

And the wood burned to embers.

And the iron keel clattered onto the hearth. (*Drops yacht*)

May God bless her and all who sail in her!

35 Star of the Sea. Stella Maris.

Amabo. I will love.

Amazin the things ye remember.

Glasgow made the Clyde, the Clyde made Glasgow.

Matter can neither be created nor destroyed.

40 Ah had a yacht

Y'ought tae see it.

DAVIE: Put it in the canal.

Ye can all see it.

(*Fade lights*)

45 (*Tape: Fats Domino, Red Sails in the Sunset*)

Questions

5. Look at lines 1–23. Explain how the language of these lines reveals the character of:

(a) Alec **4**

(b) Davie **4**

6. Look at lines 24–45. Explain how the language of these lines shows the importance of the burning of the boat. **4**

7. By referring to this extract and elsewhere in the play, show how the play deals with the theme of family relationships. **8**

OR

Text 3 — Drama

If you choose this text, you may not attempt a question on Drama in Section 2.

Read the extract below and then attempt the following questions.

***Tally's Blood* by Ann Marie Di Mambro**

Hughie on his own (e.g. taking eyes out of potatoes).

Lucia in.

LUCIA: Hello, Hughie

Hughie looks up: delighted.

5 HUGHIE: Lucia! I never saw you come in. You staying long?

LUCIA: No, I'm just passing. I came in to get some money for the shopping.

HUGHIE: I bet you're going to buy something nice to wear.

LUCIA: I wish I was. I've to get something for tonight's dinner.

HUGHIE: You?

10 LUCIA: I know. Don't laugh. I'm doing the cooking these days. Auntie Rosinella says I've to learn to look after the house. Don't ask me why.

HUGHIE: Do you like it?

LUCIA: I hate it.

HUGHIE: Lucia?

15 LUCIA: Hughie?

HUGHIE: Lucia?

LUCIA: Hughie?

HUGHIE: I wish you wouldn't do that –

LUCIA: I'm sorry. What is it?

20 *Hughie goes to his jacket: takes out an envelope: gives it to her.*

LUCIA: What's this?

HUGHIE: Just a letter. I've had it for a few days – I wasn't sure when I'd see you.

She goes to open it. He stops her.

HUGHIE: Not here.

25 *Lucia looks searchingly at him:*

Rosinella in: Lucia pockets the letter hastily:

Rosinella annoyed when she sees the two of them together.

ROSINELLA: What you doing here, Lucia?

LUCIA: I came to get some money.

30 ROSINELLA: You finished those potatoes yet, Hughie?

HUGHIE: Aye

ROSINELLA: Then go and set the tables.

HUGHIE: I've done that.

ROSINELLA: Then go and find something else to do.

35 *Hughie hovers, looks at Lucia, then goes.*

ROSINELLA: I left money on the sideboard for the shopping.

LUCIA: I'm sick fed up stuck in that house. Why don't YOU go home and I'll work here?

ROSINELLA: Where is it?

LUCIA: Where's what?

40 ROSINELLA: Give me it.

LUCIA: What?

ROSINELLA: Fine you know. The letter.

LUCIA: What letter?

ROSINELLA: The letter he gave you. Now come on, I saw you hide it.

45 LUCIA: I never.

ROSINELLA: Give it to me.

Rosinella reaches out for Lucia's pocket, Lucia pulls back and takes it out herself and gives it to her. Hughie in background. Has looked in, but is not seen: he slips away.

Questions

8.   Look at lines 1–13. Using your own words as far as possible, explain what these lines show about the relationship between Lucia and Hughie.

2

9.   Look at lines 14–24. Explain how the language of these lines makes clear Hughie's feelings about the letter.

2

10. Look at lines 25–35. Explain how the language of these lines shows the tension between Hughie and Rosinella.

4

11. Look at lines 36–48 and explain how the language of these lines illustrates the relationship between Lucia and Rosinella at this point in the play.

4

12. By referring to this scene and elsewhere in the play, discuss the theme of love.

8

PART B — SCOTTISH TEXT — PROSE

Text 1 — Prose

If you choose this text, you may not attempt a question on Prose in Section 2.

Read the extract below and then attempt the following questions.

The Cone Gatherers by Robin Jenkins

'Is that you, John?' called his mother-in-law sharply from the living-room.

'Aye, it's me,' he answered, and went in.

She was seated knitting beside the wireless set. The door to Peggy's bedroom was wide open to let her too listen to the cheerful music.

5   Mrs Lochie was a stout white-haired woman, with an expression of dour resoluteness that she wore always, whether peeling potatoes or feeding hens or as at present knitting a white bedjacket. It was her intimation that never would she allow her daughter's misfortune to conquer her, but that also never would she forgive whoever was responsible for that misfortune. Even in sleep her features did not relax, as if God too was a suspect, not to be trusted.

10 'You're late,' she said, as she rose and put down her knitting. It was an accusation. 'She's been anxious about you. I'll set out your tea. '

'Thanks,' he said, and stood still.

'Aren't you going in?' she asked. 'That's her shouting for you.' She came close to him and whispered. 'Do you think I don't ken what an effort it is for you?'

15 There was no pity in her question, only condemnation; and his very glance towards the bedroom where his wife, with plaintive giggles, kept calling his name proved her right.

'It's a pity, isn't it,' whispered Mrs Lochie, with a smile, 'she doesn't die and leave you in peace?'

He did not deny her insinuation, nor did he try to explain to her that love itself perhaps could become paralysed.

20 'Take care, though, ' she muttered, as she went away, 'you don't let her see it.'

With a shudder he walked over and stood in the doorway of the bedroom.

Peggy was propped up on pillows, and was busy chewing. The sweetness of her youth still haunting amidst the great wobbling masses of pallid fat that composed her face added to her grotesqueness a pathos that often had visitors bursting into unexpected tears. She loved children
25 but they were terrified by her; she would for hours dandle a pillow as if it was a baby. Her hair was still wonderfully black and glossy, so that she insisted on wearing it down about her shoulders, bound with red ribbons. White though was her favourite colour. Her nightdresses, with lace at neck and sleeves, were always white and fresh and carefully ironed. When she had been well, in the first two years of their marriage, she had loved to race with him hand in hand over moor and
30 field, through whins and briers, up knolls and hills to the clouds: any old skirt and jumper had done then.

Though not capable of conveying it well, either by word or expression, she was pleased and relieved to see him home. Her voice was squeaky with an inveterate petulance, although sometimes, disconcerting everybody who heard it, her old gay laughter could suddenly burst
35 forth, followed by tears of wonder and regret.

He stood by the door.

'Am I to get a kiss?' she asked.

'I've still to wash, Peggy. I've been in the wood, handling rabbits.'

'I don't care. Amn't I a gamekeeper's wife? I used to like the smell of rabbits. I want a kiss.'

Questions

13. Using your own words as far as possible, explain Duror's feelings during this extract. |4

14. Look at lines 1–21 and explain how **two** examples of language give a clear impression of the character of Mrs Lochie. |4

15. Look at lines 22–39. Explain how **two** examples of language make clear the character of Peggy both now **and** before her illness. |4

16. By referring to this extract and elsewhere in the novel, show how characters are shown to be distant and / or disconnected from one another. |8

OR

Text 2 — Prose

If you choose this text, you may not attempt a question on Prose in Section 2.

Read the extract below and then attempt the following questions.

The Strange Case of Dr Jekyll and Mr Hyde by Robert Louis Stevenson

The scud had banked over the moon, and it was now quite dark. The wind, which only broke in puffs and draughts into that deep well of building, tossed the light of the candle to and fro about their steps, until they came into the shelter of the theatre, where they sat down silently to wait. London hummed solemnly all around; but nearer at hand, the stillness was only broken by the
5   sounds of a footfall moving to and fro along the cabinet floor.

"So it will walk all day, sir," whispered Poole; "ay, and the better part of the night. Only when a new sample comes from the chemist, there's a bit of a break. Ah, it's an ill conscience that's such an enemy to rest! Ah, sir, there's blood foully shed in every step of it! But hark again, a little closer— put your heart in your ears, Mr. Utterson, and tell me, is that the doctor's foot?"

10   The steps fell lightly and oddly, with a certain swing, for all they went so slowly; it was different indeed from the heavy creaking tread of Henry Jekyll. Utterson sighed. "Is there never anything else?" he asked.

Poole nodded. "Once," he said. "Once I heard it weeping!"

"Weeping? how that?" said the lawyer, conscious of a sudden chill of horror.

15   "Weeping like a woman or a lost soul," said the butler. "I came away with that upon my heart, that I could have wept too."

But now the ten minutes drew to an end. Poole disinterred the axe from under a stack of packing straw; the candle was set upon the nearest table to light them to the attack; and they drew near with bated breath to where that patient foot was still going up and down, up and down, in the
20   quiet of the night. "Jekyll," cried Utterson, with a loud voice, "I demand to see you." He paused a moment, but there came no reply. "I give you fair warning, our suspicions are aroused, and I must and shall see you," he resumed; "if not by fair means, then by foul—if not of your consent, then by brute force!"

"Utterson," said the voice, "for God's sake, have mercy!"

25   "Ah, that's not Jekyll's voice—it's Hyde's!" cried Utterson. "Down with the door, Poole!"

Poole swung the axe over his shoulder; the blow shook the building, and the red baize door leaped against the lock and hinges. A dismal screech, as of mere animal terror, rang from the cabinet. Up went the axe again, and again the panels crashed and the frame bounded; four times the blow fell; but the wood was tough and the fittings were of excellent workmanship; and it was
30   not until the fifth, that the lock burst and the wreck of the door fell inwards on the carpet.

The besiegers, appalled by their own riot and the stillness that had succeeded, stood back a little and peered in. There lay the cabinet before their eyes in the quiet lamplight, a good fire glowing and chattering on the hearth, the kettle singing its thin strain, a drawer or two open, papers neatly set forth on the business table, and nearer the fire, the things laid out for tea; the
35 quietest room, you would have said, and, but for the glazed presses full of chemicals, the most commonplace that night in London.

Right in the middle there lay the body of a man sorely contorted and still twitching. They drew near on tiptoe, turned it on its back and beheld the face of Edward Hyde. He was dressed in clothes far too large for him, clothes of the doctor's bigness; the cords of his face still moved
40 with a semblance of life, but life was quite gone: and by the crushed phial in the hand and the strong smell of kernels that hung upon the air, Utterson knew that he was looking on the body of a self-destroyer.

Questions

17. Using your own words as far as possible, explain what happens in this extract from the novel.

4

18. Look at lines 1–5 and show how **one** example of the writer's language creates atmosphere.

2

19. Look at lines 6–42 and show how **three** examples of language create tension.

6

20. By referring to this extract and elsewhere in the novel, describe the portrayal of the character of Utterson.

8

OR

Text 3 — Prose

If you choose this text, you may not attempt a question on Prose in Section 2.

Read the extract below and then attempt the following questions.

The Testament of Gideon Mack by James Robertson

'Gideon,' she said, virtually falling out of the car in her rush, 'thank God! I've been leaving messages and trying to phone you all day. I thought you might be sleeping. Then I thought you might be lying dead on the kitchen floor. Are you all right?'

5 She hugged me, and I hugged her back. It was the least I could do. Jasper was in the car, and she let him out so he could thank me in person for saving his life. He did this by throwing himself at my chest, causing me to stagger backwards. When he'd calmed down we went into the manse and through to the kitchen. I put the kettle on. Lorna expressed concern about my limp. I told her it was nothing.

10 'I'll never, ever be able to thank you enough,' she said, 'you shouldn't have done it but you did, and I'm so, so grateful. Can you imagine what it's been like? I blamed myself, I blamed Jasper, I blamed you. It's been a total nightmare. I even blamed God. And then on Tuesday, when they said you'd been found! I mean, the joy! The sheer joy of it, Gideon!'

'I really didn't mean to put you through all that,' I said.

15 We had to go over everything, from the moment Jasper saw the rabbit to the phone call she'd received telling her I was alive. At first I played it as I had with McAllister, claiming memory loss for most of the three days. But Lorna was more persistent and gradually she got more out of me. I told her about what Bill Winnyford had called my NDE, and this led me to describe the first tunnel I'd been in, and then the pool, and then the cave. She listened intently.

20 'This is amazing, Gideon. Don't you see how important this is? You were so close to death. You saw what it was like. You weren't frightened until you started to come back. And the light … It's what people always hope it'll be like, but fear it won't be. Not outer darkness, but bright, eternal light. But it's even better than that: God didn't want you to die then. He sent you back to us.'

I remembered my friend's words: no more games. I bit the bullet. 'No, Lorna,' I said. 'It wasn't God who sent me back. It was the Devil.'

25 So I told her. Or rather, I went and got the cassette-recorder and rewound the tape and played it to her. We sat and listened to this voice that was mine and yet wasn't mine talking about my three days with the Devil. We might have been listening to a ghost story on an audio-book, but I knew we weren't. Jasper snoozed on the floor with his nose between his paws. The light began to go outside. We listened on, right to the end.

30 I switched off the machine. I told Lorna that the Devil had taken me out in the boat the next morning, hit me over the head with the paddle, stolen my boots and flung me back in the river. I didn't tell her that I'd arranged another meeting with him.

'I feel like I need a drink,' she said.

'I've got wine,' I said. That was all she drank, white wine. Two glasses made her squiffy.

35 'No, thanks. Not a good idea. I need to drive home.'

'There's plenty of room here,' I said, 'if you want to stay.' I said it in all innocence. I don't know why I did: I'd never suggested it before and I didn't want her to stay. She looked at me sadly, as if I'd suggested we go to bed together. As if I'd made the offer too late.

'No, I have to go. Gideon, you must promise me something.'

40 'What's that?'

'Don't tell anybody else about this. What I've just heard ... Gideon, it's mad. It's completely and utterly mad. It's also deluded, foolish, unpleasant and blasphemous. You're not well. You're clearly not well at all.'

'I'm completely well, Lorna,' I said. 'I'm tired, that's all. How can it be blasphemous? It's the truth.
45 There isn't a word of a lie in what you've heard.'

'Of course it's blasphemous. It goes against everything we stand for. You simply mustn't repeat it.'

'I can't not. I have to. It's what happened.'

Questions

21. Look at lines 1–12 and explain how **two** examples of the writer's language show Lorna's feelings at this point in the novel.

4

22. Look at lines 14–32. Explain how **two** examples of language make clear aspects of Lorna's character.

4

23. Look at lines 34–48. Using your own words as far as possible, explain how Gideon and Lorna respond to Gideon letting Lorna know about his experience with the devil.

4

24. By referring to this extract and elsewhere in the novel, explain the importance of Gideon's relationships with women.

8

OR

Text 4 — Prose

If you choose this text, you may not attempt a question on Prose in Section 2.

Read the extract below and then attempt the following questions.

Mother and Son by Iain Crichton Smith

The clock struck five wheezingly and, at the first chime, the woman woke up. She started as she saw the figure crouched over the fire and then subsided: 'It's only you.' There was relief in the voice, but there was a curious hint of contempt or acceptance. He still sat staring into the fire and answered dully: 'Yes, it's only me!' He couldn't be said to speak the words: they fell away from him
5   as sometimes happens when one is in a deep reverie where every question is met by its answer almost instinctively.

'Well, what's the matter with you!' she snapped pettishly, 'sitting there moping with the tea to be made. I sometimes don't know why we christened you John' – with a sigh. 'My father was never like you. He was a man who knew his business.'

10 'All right, all right,' he said despairingly. 'Can't you get a new record for your gramophone. I've heard all that before,' as if he were conscious of the inadequacy of this familiar retort – he added: 'hundreds of times.' But she wasn't to be stopped.

'I can't understand what has come over you lately. You keep mooning about the house, pacing up and down with your hands in your pockets. Do you know what's going to happen to you, you'll be
15 taken to the asylum. That's where you'll go. Your father's people had something wrong with their heads, it was in your family but not in ours.' (She had always looked upon him as her husband's son, not as her own: and all his faults she attributed to hereditary weaknesses on his father's side.)

He pottered about, putting water in the kettle, waiting desperately for the sibilant noise to stop. But no, it took a long time to stop. He moved about inside this sea of sound trying to keep
20 detached, trying to force himself from listening. Sometimes, at rarer and rarer intervals, he could halt and watch her out of a clear, cold mind as if she didn't matter, as if her chatter which eddied round and round, then burst venomously towards him, had no meaning for him, could not touch him. At these times her little bitter barbs passed over him or through him to come out on the other side. Most often however they stung him and stood quivering in his flesh, and he would say
25 something angrily with the reflex of the wound. But she always cornered him. She had so much patience, and then again she enjoyed pricking him with her subtle arrows. He had now become so sensitive that he usually read some devilish meaning into her smallest utterance.

'Have you stacked all the sheaves now?' she was asking. He swung round on his eddying island as if he had seen that the seas were relenting, drawing back. At such moments he became
30 deferential.

'Yes,' he said joyously. 'I've stacked them all. And I've done it all alone too. I did think Roddy Mason would help. But he doesn't seem to have much use for me now. He's gone the way the rest of the boys go. They all take a job. Then they get together and laugh at me.' His weakness was pitiful: his childish blue eyes brimmed with tears. Into the grimace by which he sought to tauten his face,

35   he put a murderous determination: but though the lines of his face were hard, the eyes had no steadiness: the last dominance had long faded and lost itself in the little red lines which crossed and recrossed like a graph.

Questions

25. Look at lines 1–17. Explain how **two** examples of language make clear the relationship between John and his mother.

4

26. Look at lines 18–27. Explain how **two** examples of language show John's response to his mother's cruelty.

4

27. Look at lines 28–37 and explain how **two** examples of language make clear John's feelings.

4

28. By referring to this story and at least **one** other by Crichton Smith, discuss how his stories give an insight into characters' feelings.

8

OR

Text 5 — Prose

If you choose this text, you may not attempt a question on Prose in Section 2.

Read the extract below and then attempt the following questions.

Dear Santa by Anne Donovan

Ma mammy disnae love me. Ah kin see it in her eyes, no the way she looks at me, but the way she looks through me, the way you look at sumpn that's been in the hoose fur years; you know it's there but you don't see it. It's hard no tae be seen. It makes you wee and crumpled up inside. When ah kiss her on the cheek, her skin creases, soft and squashy lik a marshmallow, and close up
5 ah see the lines runnin doon the sidey her mooth and smell the powder on her face. She doesnae kiss me back.

You kin read fur ten minutes but then that light's tae be aff.

Gonnae come and tuck me in, Mammy?

You're too big tae be tucked in.

10 She keeps watchin the television.

You tuck Katie in.

Katie's only five. You're a big girl.

Ah'm eight year auld. Ah'm a big girl.

Ah don't know if ma mammy loved me afore Katie wis born, ah cannae mind that fur back but ah
15 must of been jealous when she was wee. Ah remember wan day she wis lyin sleepin in her pram ootside and ah got plastercine and made it intae wee balls and stuck them all ower her face: she looked as if she had some horrible disease. Ah mind staunin there lookin doon at that soft skin covered in sticky horrible purple lumps and felt good inside. Warm and full.

Katie's asleep in the other bed, fair curly hair spread oot across the pillow. Smilin in her sleep the
20 way she does when she's awake. Ma sister is perfect, ah kin see that, she's wee and pretty and aye happy, bubblin ower wi life. When the sun shines, she's runnin aboot the gairden efter sunbeams and when it rains she pits on her wellies and splashes in the puddles. She never cries. Ma daddy says she's a princess, her teacher says she's an angel. Ma mammy says,

Why can't you be more like your sister?

25 In the school nativity play Katie gets picked as the angel that tells Mary she's gonnae huv the baby Jesus so ma mammy sits up all night sewin her a white robe and a perra golden wings. Ah'm a shepherd. Wi a stripy tea towel roon ma heid. In the photy she's at the front, in between Mary and Joseph, glitterin as if she really wis an angel, and ah'm this big lurkin thing at the endy the back row. Daurk and blurred.

30 The photy gets framed and put on the unit in the livin room.

Questions

29. Look at lines 1–13 and explain how **two** examples of language make clear Alison's feelings.

4

30. Look at lines 14–18. Explain how **two** examples of language show Alison's jealousy of her sister.

4

31. Look at lines 19–30. Explain how **two** examples of language create contrast between Alison and her sister.

4

32. By referring to this story and at least **one** other by Anne Donovan, discuss how she portrays the theme of relationships.

8

PART C — SCOTTISH TEXT — POETRY

Text 1 — Poetry

If you choose this text, you may not attempt a question on Poetry in Section 2.

Read the extract below and then attempt the following questions.

***Mrs Midas* by Carol Ann Duffy**

And who, when it comes to the crunch, can live

with a heart of gold? That night, I dreamt I bore

his child, its perfect ore limbs, its little tongue

like a precious latch, its amber eyes

5   holding their pupils like flies. My dream milk

burned in my breasts. I woke to the streaming sun.

So he had to move out. We'd a caravan

in the wilds, in a glade of its own. I drove him up

under the cover of dark. He sat in the back.

10   And then I came home, the woman who married the fool

who wished for gold. At first, I visited, odd times,

parking the car a good way off, then walking.

You knew you were getting close. Golden trout

on the grass. One day, a hare hung from a larch,

15   a beautiful lemon mistake. And then his footprints,

glistening next to the river's path. He was thin,

delirious; hearing, he said, the music of Pan

from the woods. Listen. That was the last straw.

What gets me now is not the idiocy or greed

20   but lack of thought for me. Pure selfishness. I sold

the contents of the house and came down here.

I think of him in certain lights, dawn, late afternoon,

and once a bowl of apples stopped me dead. I miss most,

even now, his hands, his warm hands on my skin, his touch.

Questions

33. Look at lines 1–6. By referring to **two** examples of language, explain how the poet makes clear Mrs Midas' feelings.   **4**

34. Look at lines 7–18. By referring to **two** examples of language, explain how the poet shows Mrs Midas' reaction to her husband.   **4**

35. Look at lines 19–24. By referring to **two** examples of language, explain why these lines are an effective conclusion to the poem.   **4**

36. By referring to this poem and at least **one** other by Duffy, describe how she gives an insight into characters' thoughts and feelings.   **8**

OR

Text 2 — Poetry

If you choose this text, you may not attempt a question on Poetry in Section 2.

Read the poem below and then attempt the following questions.

***Glasgow Sonnet* by Edwin Morgan**

A mean wind wanders through the backcourt trash.

Hackles on puddles rise, old mattresses

puff briefly and subside. Play-fortresses

of brick and bric-a-brac spill out some ash.

5   Four storeys have no windows left to smash,

but the fifth a chipped sill buttresses

mother and daughter the last mistresses

of that black block condemned to stand, not crash.

Around them the cracks deepen, the rats crawl.

10 The kettle whimpers on a crazy hob.

Roses of mould grow from ceiling to wall.

The man lies late since he has lost his job,

smokes on one elbow, letting his coughs fall

thinly into an air too poor to rob.

Questions

37. Look at lines 1–4. By referring to **two** examples of language, explain how the poet creates setting effectively.

4

38. Look at lines 5–8. By referring to **two** examples of language, explain how the poet portrays the poverty of this place.

4

39. Look at lines 9–14. By referring to **two** examples of language, explain how the poet conveys the theme of poverty.

4

40. By referring to this poem and at least **one** other by Morgan, describe how the poet describes how people respond to their surroundings or their experiences.

8

OR

Text 3 — Poetry

If you choose this text, you may not attempt a question on Poetry in Section 2.

Read the poem below and then attempt the following questions.

***Hotel Room, 12th Floor* by Norman MacCaig**

This morning I watched from here

a helicopter skirting like a damaged insect

the Empire State building, that

jumbo size dentist's drill, and landing

5   on the roof of the PanAm skyscraper.

But now Midnight has come in

from foreign places. Its uncivilised darkness

is shot at by a million lit windows, all

ups and acrosses.

10 But midnight is not

so easily defeated. I lie in bed, between

a radio and a television set, and hear

the wildest of warwhoops continually ululating through

the glittering canyons and gulches –

15 police cars and ambulances racing

to broken bones, the harsh screaming

from coldwater flats, the blood

glazed on sidewalks.

The frontier is never

20 somewhere else. And no stockades

can keep the midnight out.

Questions

41. Look at lines 1–9. By referring to **three** examples of language, explain how the poet portrays his response to New York.

6

42. Look at lines 10–18. By referring to **two** examples of language, explain how the poet conveys his troubled feelings.

4

43. Look at lines 19–21. By referring to **one** example of language, explain why this is an effective conclusion to the poem.

2

44. By referring to this poem and at least **one** other poem by MacCaig, explain how his poetry responds to significant experiences.

8

OR

Text 4 — Poetry

If you choose this text, you may not attempt a question on Poetry in Section 2.

Read the extract below and then attempt the following questions.

***Gap Year (for Mateo)* by Jackie Kay**

You started the Inca trail in Arctic conditions

and ended up in subtropical. Now you plan the Amazon

in Bolivia. Your grandfather rings again to say

'There's three warring factions in Bolivia, warn him

5   against it. He canny see everything. Tell him to come home.'

But you say all the travellers you meet rave about Bolivia. You want

to see the Salar de Uyuni,

the world's largest salt-flats, the Amazonian rainforest.

And now you are not coming home till four weeks after

10 your due date. After Bolivia, you plan to stay

with a friend's Auntie in Argentina.

Then – to Chile where you'll stay with friends of Diane's.

And maybe work for the Victor Jara Foundation.

I feel like a home-alone mother; all the lights

15 have gone out in the hall, and now I am

wearing your large black slippers, flip-flopping

into your empty bedroom, trying to imagine you

in your bed. I stare at the photos you send by messenger:

you on the top of the world, arms outstretched, eager.

20 Blue sky, white snow; you by Lake Tararhua, beaming.

My heart soars like the birds in your bright blue skies.

My love glows like the sunrise over the lost city.

I sing along to Ella Fitzgerald, A tisket A tasket.

I have a son out in the big wide world.

25   A flip and a skip ago, you were dreaming in your basket.

Questions

45. Look at lines 1–12. Explain how **two** examples of language make clear her attitude towards her son's travels.   **4**

46. Look at lines 13–20 and explain how **two** examples of language show how the mother feels.   **4**

47. Look at lines 21–25 and explain how the language shows how her feelings change in the closing lines of the poem.   **4**

48. By referring to this poem and at least **one** other by Kay, explain how she describes people dealing with difficult circumstances.   **8**

SECTION 2 — CRITICAL ESSAY — 20 marks

Attempt ONE question from the following genres — Drama, Prose, Poetry, Film and Television Drama, or Language. Your answer must be on a different genre from that chosen in Section 1. You should spend approximately 45 minutes on this Section.

DRAMA

Answers to questions in this part should refer to the text and to such relevant features as characterisation, key scene(s), structure, climax, theme, plot, conflict, setting …

1. Choose a play that has a scene that is vital to the play as a whole.

   By referring to appropriate dramatic techniques, describe how the writer makes clear why this scene is vital.

2. Choose a play that has a fascinating character.

   By referring to appropriate dramatic techniques, describe what is fascinating about this character.

PROSE

Answers to questions in this part should refer to the text and to such relevant features as characterisation, setting, language, key incident(s), climax, turning point, plot, structure, narrative technique, theme, ideas, description …

3. Choose a novel or a short story or a work of non-fiction in which setting in time and / or place is an important feature.

   By referring to appropriate techniques, show how the writer describes the setting and discuss why it is important to the text as a whole.

4. Choose a novel or a short story that has a character who creates a strong response in the audience.

   By referring to appropriate techniques, show how the writer makes this relationship interesting.

POETRY

Answers to questions in this part should refer to the text and to such relevant features as word choice, tone, imagery, structure, content, rhythm, rhyme, theme, sound, ideas …

5. Choose a poem which deals with an important theme.

   By referring to poetic techniques, explain how the importance of this theme is conveyed by the poet.

6. Choose a poem that is shocking or surprising or inspiring.

   By referring to poetic techniques, explain how the poem creates this emotion.

FILM AND TELEVISION DRAMA*

Answers to questions in this part should refer to the text and to such relevant features as use of camera, key sequence, characterisation, mise-en-scène, editing, setting, music / sound, special effects, plot, dialogue …

7. Choose a scene or a sequence from a film or TV drama that is important to the fate of the main character.

   Explain why the sequence is important and by referring to appropriate techniques, explain how the importance is made clear.

8. Choose a film or TV drama that has a main character that creates a mixed response in the audience.

   By referring to appropriate techniques, explain how this mixed response is created.

* 'TV drama' includes a single play, a series or a serial.

LANGUAGE

Answers to questions in this part should refer to the text and to such relevant features as register, accent, dialect, slang, jargon, vocabulary, tone, abbreviation …

9. Choose **two** adverts that use persuasive language.

   By referring to specific examples from the advertisement, compare the ways that they use language to persuade.

10. Consider a group of people who use language in a particular way.

    By referring to specific examples, explain how the language of the group is particular to them.

[END OF QUESTION PAPER]